Cambridge Elements

Elements in Public Economics
edited by
Robin Boadway
Queen's University
Frank A. Cowell
The London School of Economics and Political Science
Massimo Florio
University of Milan

STATE-OWNED ENTERPRISES IN DEVELOPED MARKET ECONOMIES

Theory and Empirics

Chiara F. Del Bo
University of Milan

Massimo Florio
University of Milan

Marco Frigerio
University of Siena

Daniela Vandone
University of Milan

CAMBRIDGE
UNIVERSITY PRESS

CAMBRIDGE
UNIVERSITY PRESS

Shaftesbury Road, Cambridge CB2 8EA, United Kingdom

One Liberty Plaza, 20th Floor, New York, NY 10006, USA

477 Williamstown Road, Port Melbourne, VIC 3207, Australia

314–321, 3rd Floor, Plot 3, Splendor Forum, Jasola District Centre,
New Delhi – 110025, India

103 Penang Road, #05–06/07, Visioncrest Commercial, Singapore 238467

Cambridge University Press is part of Cambridge University Press & Assessment,
a department of the University of Cambridge.

We share the University's mission to contribute to society through the pursuit
of education, learning and research at the highest international levels of excellence.

www.cambridge.org
Information on this title: www.cambridge.org/9781009625258

DOI: 10.1017/9781009625265

© Chiara F. Del Bo, Massimo Florio, Marco Frigerio and Daniela Vandone 2025

This publication is in copyright. Subject to statutory exception and to the provisions
of relevant collective licensing agreements, no reproduction of any part may take
place without the written permission of Cambridge University Press & Assessment.

When citing this work, please include a reference to the DOI 10.1017/9781009625265

First published 2025

A catalogue record for this publication is available from the British Library

ISBN 978-1-009-62525-8 Hardback
ISBN 978-1-009-62522-7 Paperback
ISSN 2516-2276 (online)
ISSN 2516-2268 (print)

Cambridge University Press & Assessment has no responsibility for the persistence
or accuracy of URLs for external or third-party internet websites referred to in this
publication and does not guarantee that any content on such websites is, or will
remain, accurate or appropriate.

State-Owned Enterprises in Developed Market Economies

Theory and Empirics

Elements in Public Economics

DOI: 10.1017/9781009625265
First published online: January 2025

Chiara F. Del Bo
University of Milan

Massimo Florio
University of Milan

Marco Frigerio
University of Siena

Daniela Vandone
University of Milan

Author for correspondence: Massimo Florio, massimo.florio@unimi.it

Abstract: After briefly reviewing the received doctrine prior to the waves of privatizations beginning in the 1980s, this Element offers a survey of various analytical frameworks on state-owned enterprises (SOEs) from the perspective of applied welfare economics. The focus then shifts to a positive analysis of the comparative performance of private versus public enterprises, with a specific emphasis on SOEs in developed market economies over the past two decades; key metrics examined include profitability, productivity, internationalization, innovativeness, and environmental sustainability. The Element also addresses empirical methodological issues, alongside contextual conditions and institutional factors that help explain the outcomes. It reviews selected contributions from public economics, industrial organization, corporate governance, management studies, and other social sciences. Overall, the Element aims to redefine a neglected research area in public economics, considering the new circumstances of the twenty-first century, where SOEs compete with other firms in developed market economies.

Keywords: public enterprises, performance, productivity, corporate governance, public mission

JEL classifications: L32, L33, H40

© Chiara F. Del Bo, Massimo Florio, Marco Frigerio and Daniela Vandone 2025

ISBNs: 9781009625258 (HB), 9781009625227 (PB), 9781009625265 (OC)
ISSNs: 2516-2276 (online), 2516-2268 (print)

Contents

1 Introduction — 1

2 Normative Theory — 4

3 Empirics — 24

4 Concluding Remarks — 70

   References — 74

1 Introduction

This Cambridge Element reviews selected analytical and empirical issues related to the re-emergence of public enterprises (henceforth referred to as state-owned enterprises, SOEs) at the turn of the century, following decades of privatizations. Currently, there are different forms of SOEs: fully state-owned, state-invested with or without government control, municipal/local service providers, development banks and other government-owned/sponsored financial entities, international organizations with industrial or research policy missions, and others. Their size may vary from very small units, such as those in charge of waste management in rural towns, to giants like multinational oil and gas companies, investment banks, or space agencies. These organizations, while not strictly part of the public administration in legal terms, are ultimately controlled or partly controlled by a government through its ownership rights and are embedded, formally or de facto, in public policy frameworks. Why do SOEs exist? What do they do differently from private enterprises? How should governments balance between too close and too lax control of their missions, management, and results?

Context and history are relevant in answering these questions. Historically, in some developed market economies, governments created SOEs primarily in industries (such as telecoms, electricity, water, and sewerage) where private investment was insufficient. In other cases, governments wanted to rescue financially fragile and bankrupt, but otherwise essential, firms. According to economic historians, particularly Millward (2013), military concerns were paramount (e.g., railways in France and Germany). When a social democratic party was in power, additional ideological drivers were also important, but concerns for social cohesion or national prestige were often shared by right-wing politicians as well. In developing countries, additional motivations included freeing the country from previous colonial ownership and catching up with the developed world at an accelerated pace. In other words, SOEs have always been creatures of historical circumstance, usually coupled with ideological drivers (as a reviewer of this Element has duly reminded us).

In a dramatic policy reversal, privatizations between the 1980s and the end of the last century were motivated by a mixture of efficiency arguments, financial considerations, and ideology (see Vickers and Yarrow 1988, Newbery 2000, Megginson and Netter 2001, Florio 2004, 2013, Roland 2008). Our main focus here, however, is not on earlier nationalizations or privatizations in the twentieth century. Instead, we are interested in discussing the rationales and performance of contemporary SOEs that survived earlier privatization waves and that, contrary to common belief, often fared well in developed market economies.

Several research areas arise from earlier literature on SOEs (see World Bank 1994, Bayliss and Fine 1998, OECD 2006, CEEP 2010, Hefetz and Warner 2011, Bernier et al. 2020b); in this Element, we are particularly interested in redefining the role and performance of SOEs in terms of broad policy agendas (e.g., energy transition and climate change, innovation policy, long-term sustainability of the welfare state). We are also interested in tensions or complementarities between such agendas and internationalization; the relationship between the quality of institutions, corporate governance, and social accountability (including the role of citizens); and new governance mechanisms. While the present Element cannot fully cover all the established and emerging topics, we will discuss the most relevant ones for the future research agenda and for designing public policies and institutional settings.

As with any topic in social sciences, it is useful to clarify whether the research perspective is mainly normative or positive. In the latter case, the study object should be described in terms of real-world circumstances, which usually implies an effort of classification and suitable abstraction. In the former perspective, one needs to start from a relatively abstract model and then discuss to what extent it may fit with real-world circumstances. In this Element, we analyze SOEs from both perspectives, respectively in Section 2 and Section 3.

A caveat: the current literature on public enterprises or SOEs often takes stock of earlier contributions, mainly by European scholars, over two centuries (from 'municipal socialism' in the UK and Italy, *régies nationales* in France, *Gemeinwirtschaft* organizations in Germany, to the 'nationalized industries' and 'public corporations'). Later on, there were three decades of research on privatization policy, mainly spanning from the late 1980s to the 2000s. Eventually, particularly after the Great Recession (2008), there has been considerable interest in public enterprises, both at the national level (in some cases as a consequence of government bailout operations of bankrupted private companies) or at the international level (in many cases with the transformation of 'national champions' into multinational corporations). Given the long history of this literature and its global dimension, we need to highlight the boundaries of our research:

1. We do not consider economic organizations developed in planned economies along the Soviet model and the related 'soft-budget constraints' literature (Kornai 1980, Stiglitz 1994, Maskin 1996). In that context, an SOE was typically a production unit with top-down objectives set by planners or other relevant policymakers. Choices in terms of product portfolio, quality and quantity, procurement, hiring of personnel, and prices were determined by the circumstances of a planned economy. This context is out

of our scope. Interested readers are referred, for example, to Estrin et al. (2009) for a survey.
2. We do not present a history of the origins, rise, and fall of SOEs in capitalist economies: there are excellent literature review papers and books (see e.g., Millward 2007, 2013, Toninelli 2011). We thus limit our time horizon to the past two decades and concentrate on the literature from this period. This time span approximately covers ten years before and ten years after the Great Recession, which was, as already mentioned, a turning point for SOEs in developed economies.
3. We limit our analysis to OECD countries. This, unfortunately, leaves aside China, which is of paramount importance for our topic (Chinese SOEs were valued at 29.2 USD trillion with 20.2 million employees, according to OECD, 2017). Similar limitations apply to SOEs in Russia, the Arab countries (such as the oil and gas giants), India, and elsewhere. While potentially interesting and relevant, an in-depth proper analysis in these countries would lead us to examine widely different institutional contexts. Moreover, lack of appropriate data for systematic comparability suggests referring the reader to specialized sources (see, for example, Goldstein 2013a, 2013b, Nölke 2014, Robinson 2015, Lin et al. 2020, Lin 2021, Estrin and Pelletier 2018).
4. Financial institutions such as central banks, sovereign wealth funds, public pension funds, international and national development banks, and other banks owned by governments are not examined in this Element. The inclusion of these players would necessitate a discussion of the functioning of financial markets, which is very different from the markets for goods and other services, and would merit specific treatment. Readers may refer to Cornett et al. 2010, Lazzarini et al. 2015, Frigerio and Vandone 2020, Eslava and Freixas 2021, and Clò et al. 2022 for research on SOEs in financial markets.

Within these boundaries, our research question is as follows: what are the arguments for the existence and explanations for the performance of contemporary SOEs in developed market economies (such as those in the OECD countries) and in non-financial sectors (such as energy, telecoms, transport, education, health provision, space economy, etc.)?

This Element is organized into two sections, focusing respectively on normative theory (Section 2) and empirics (Section 3). Section 2, after defining an ideal-type SOE and reviewing the received doctrine (i.e., as it was before the waves of privatizations in the 1980s and beyond), argues that such earlier contributions are now less relevant and discusses a selection of analytical frameworks for normative analysis, broadly through the lenses of applied welfare economics. Section 3 turns to positive analysis: it reviews the scholarly literature on the comparative performance of private versus public enterprises in developed countries over the past twenty years, focusing on methodological issues along with context conditions and institutional factors. Part of Section 3 deals with the role of SOE governance mechanisms in setting, implementing, and monitoring corporate strategy and discusses the need for disclosure, transparency, and accountability. Policy implications are briefly mentioned in our Concluding Remarks.

Overall, about 250 contributions are considered here, out of a literature comprising several thousand sources (e.g., about 7,000 results for 'state-owned enterprises', 12,000 for 'public enterprises' in the database IDEAS/REPEC). The selection was made with the aforementioned boundaries in mind, while striving to represent the core research topics in our discussion.

2 Normative Theory

2.1 Definition of an SOE 'Ideal-Type'

A positive or empirical definition of an SOE would require collecting information on different types of economic organizations (Thynne 2021) and eventually propose a classification that describes such observations. The OECD (2015a, 2024), in its *Guidelines on SOE Corporate Governance*, uses this definition:

> Defining an SOE. Any undertaking recognized by national law as an enterprise, and in which the state exercises ownership or control, should be considered as an SOE. This includes joint stock companies, limited liability companies, and partnerships limited by shares. Moreover, statutory corporations, with their legal personality established through specific legislation, should be considered as SOEs if their purpose and activities, or large parts of their activities, are of an economic nature.

This definition may be empirically helpful as a generic description, but it is somewhat of a truism: an SOE is simply an enterprise owned by the state. In this Element, for the purposes of normative theory, we prefer the definition provided by Bernier et al. (2020a, p. 2), in *The Routledge Handbook of State-Owned Enterprises*: an SOE is an organization that (a) directly produces public services or goods either through liberalized market arrangements or under a franchised monopoly, (b) is ultimately owned or de facto controlled by public sector entities, (c) has a public mission, (d) whose ownership in principle can be shifted to the private sector, and (e) has budgetary autonomy and managerial discretion.

We focus now on the normative dimensions implied by this definition, and their relations with earlier economic literature. Firstly, however, let us consider the meaning of 'enterprise'. In English, there are two possible meanings: 'an organization, especially a business, or a difficult and important plan, especially one that will earn money'. Examples given in the Cambridge Dictionary include a state-owned enterprise, a commercial enterprise, the spirit of competition and free enterprise, a government-sponsored enterprise, and a charitable enterprise. Some of these examples are quite distinct from something 'that will earn money'. There is a dual meaning: on one side, there is an organization, while on the other, a plan. The Oxford Dictionary provides this definition of 'enterprise': 'undertaking, esp. bold or difficult one (FREE *enterprise,* PRIVATE *enterprise*); business firm; courage; readiness, to engage in enterprises'.[1]

Interestingly, this dualism has a common root in the Latin *imprehendere*, where 'im' stands for 'in' and 'prehendere' means 'to take," together meaning 'to take inside'.[2]

Economic theory, at its highest level of abstraction, ignores this semantic duality between an organization with a purpose and the effort to implement a plan or project. As is well-known, but worth reiterating, in the Arrow–Debreu general equilibrium model of the economy, a firm is simply an atomistic unit acquiring certain inputs and transforming them into outputs. This abstract firm cannot be anything other than 'private', as there is no role for government in an Arrow–Debreu economy (with lump-sum 'taxation' in some versions of the second theorem not really implying a government, being simply a mathematical adjustment of initial conditions). Thus, whilst a given firm in such an economy can be owned by a single individual or jointly by all individuals, this would be entirely immaterial: the solutions of the systems of equations in terms of quantities and prices would remain unaffected. This firm has no mission attached to ownership, except profit maximization. The algorithm for cost minimization would lead to solutions in terms of quantity and price that are indistinguishable for a company owned by an individual or jointly by all of them. Thus, at this level of abstraction, a firm is neither a proper organization nor an enterprise (with a semantic reminder that managerial effort, beyond its use of inputs, is needed to design and implement a project). See Box 1 for a clarification of this point.

---

[1] *The Concise Oxford Dictionary of Current English*, 7th edn ed, J. B. Sykes, Clarendon Press 1982.
[2] Bianchi (2012) (online), www.treccani.it/enciclopedia/impresa_%28Dizionario-di-Economia-e-Finanza%29.

> **BOX 1 SOEs IN AN ARROW–DEBREU ECONOMY MUST BEHAVE AS PRIVATE FIRMS**
>
> In the economy there are goods $i = 1,\ldots,I$; consumers $h = 1,\ldots,H$. Consumption plans are $x^h = (x_1^h, x_2^h, \ldots, x_I^h)$ and each h has a utility function $U^h = U^h(x^h)$. Firms are $j = 1, \ldots, J$. Feasible production plans are $y^j = (y_1^j, y_2^j, \ldots, y_I^j)$. d is a vector of *ownership shares* assigning to each consumer h the net product of every j: $d_j^h = (d_1^h, d_2^h, \ldots, d_J^h)$. An SOE is defined as a firm: $r = 1, \ldots R$, included in a subset of J, s.t. $d^{hr} = 1/H$ for each h and r. In an SOE, *voting rights* are delegated to government, while profits accrue to individual shareholders. Initial endowments of consumer goods for every consumer are vectors e^h and p is the vector of the relative production prices $p = (p_1, p_2, \ldots, p_I)$. By assumption $e^h \subset R_+^I \forall h$ and $d_j^h \geq 0 \forall h$ (consumers have no negative property rights on firms, including SOEs) and $\sum_h d_j^h = 1$. Profits are $\prod^j \equiv p y^j$, distributed through shares d_j^h; this applies to SOEs as well. The hth consumer determines the optimal consumption plan x^h solving the following constrained program: $\max_{x^h} U^h(x_1^h, \ldots, x_I^h)$ subject to (s.t.) $\sum_{i=1}^H p_i x_i^h \leq \sum_{i=1}^H p_i e_i^h + \sum_{j=1}^J d_j^h \Pi^j$, $\bar{x}_- < x^h < \bar{x}_+$. Firms adopt the following program: $\max_{y^j} p y^j$ s.t. $\bar{y}_- < y^j < \bar{y}_+$. In a Walrasian equilibrium, summing up all the individual budget constraints and calling $x_i \equiv \sum_{h=1}^H x_i^h$, the net demand is null: $\sum_{i=1}^I p_i x_i = \sum_{j=1}^J \sum_{h=1}^H d_j^h \Pi^j + \sum_{h=1}^H \sum_{i=1}^I p_i e_i^h$, where p vector is for the unique equilibrium solution.
>
> The government adopts the program: $\max_{x^h} W = W[U^h(x^h)]$ s.t. the Pareto criterion. Suppose that the government instructs an SOE's manager to deviate from $\max_{y^j} p y^j$, for example to supply larger than optimal quantity of a specific good at a discount price. This would decrease the lump-sum income of all the SOE's shareholders, and hence their consumption and utility, while increasing the indirect utility of some consumers, hence prices no longer support a Walrasian equilibrium. As the latter for the first theorem of welfare economics is Pareto efficient, and government is committed to $\max W(U)$, it would contradict its own objective.
>
> Source: The authors, adapted from Florio and Pancotti (2023).

Let us now consider SOEs from the perspective of this preliminary discussion. From a positive standpoint, we observe a large variability of forms of SOEs, ranging from small municipal firms in charge of water distribution in a small jurisdiction, to giant multinational corporations extracting and processing oil globally. It is certainly possible to build a taxonomy of existing SOEs, but what differentiates an SOE from any private enterprise given their wide range of forms?

We shall argue that the answer to this question lies in a normative model, in other words, a model explaining why anything different from private enterprises should exist in the first place. To see this, the core underlying concept is: ownership by whom to do what.

There is a wide literature on the ownership rights of firms (e.g., Hansmann 2000), particularly in the law and economics tradition, hence we will not discuss in detail the specific content of these rights, including the right for the owners to be the residual claimants of profits, to appoint and fire managers, or to shut down the firm if needed, and so on. Thus, let us say that a private enterprise is an organization where the ownership rights can be effectively claimed, directly or by delegation, by individuals, and is characterized by its own objectives, usually assumed to be profit maximization.

Conversely, at this abstract level, an SOE is defined as an organization where all (or a controlling part) of the related ownership rights can be effectively claimed by a government (or a public sector) entity on behalf of all citizens, to do something that a private organization would not do or would do differently. 'Effectively' here means that the legal provisions on ownership rights should not be blocked or so diluted as to become just a misnomer for de facto something else, such as when an individual is not free or a government agent is captured by an individual interest (e.g., an oil and gas company formally 'public' but actually controlled by some oligarchs). This is our starting point for a normative model of public enterprises, inspired by the aforementioned definition by Bernier et al. (2020a), further developed and qualified as follows:

1. It is not the production of a tangible or intangible good per se that counts in the ideal-type of SOE, but rather the fact that whatever good is produced should in principle provide a 'service' to the public. Thus, the focus should be on identifying this service, understanding its rationale, and evaluating productive performance. Hence, from a normative perspective, the issue is exploring why a government should want to own or co-own an entity providing such a service. Moreover, while earlier economic literature assumed that the typical market environment for an SOE is a monopoly, the aforementioned definition extends the perspective to oligopoly and other market forms. As we shall discuss later, this dramatically changes the way a normative theory of SOEs can be designed,

for example concerning pricing rules, which were a typical object of the traditional view of economic textbooks such as Atkinson and Stiglitz (1980).
2. Ownership without control would render the SOE definition meaningless for normative analysis. From a positive perspective, ownership rights, and actual control may not always be fully aligned, but we can assume some extent of alignment. However, control may vary in meaning and intensity. From a normative perspective, the issue is defining the optimal or desirable degree of control, which relates to point (5) below.
3. Is an organization without a public mission (Sorrentino 2020) considered an SOE? Empirically, according to the definition provided by the OECD (2015a), the answer is yes. However, from our normative perspective, it is not. The default rule for an economic organization without a public mission would be to revert to cost minimization, and equivalently to profit maximization. This point has wide implications for the concept and role of a public mission as defined and attributed by a government to an economic organization.
4. The explicit possibility of privatization as part of the definition excludes from the SOE ideal-type those specific government activities that cannot be meaningfully provided by private companies, such as law-making and most judicial and cabinet core functions. Conversely, prisons, police services, hospitals, space exploration, and certain defence services, just to provide some concrete examples, have been partly privatized in some countries.
5. Any organization without its own budget is formally part of another organization. The same applies if an organization is so tightly controlled by another entity that its managers have no practical budget autonomy.

With this ideal-type in mind, we shall now discuss some relevant theoretical issues for SOEs which meet the aforementioned criteria.

2.2 Looking Back: Some Prescriptions From Earlier Public Economics Literature

Atkinson and Stiglitz (1980), unlike more recent textbooks (e.g., Hindriks and Myles 2013), allocated two chapters to public sector production. Their 'Lecture 15' discusses pricing policies by public enterprises (which are not precisely defined in the text) and justifications for deviations from the benchmark case, such as marginal cost pricing in the tradition of Hotelling. The argument is based on the analogy between optimal taxation and public enterprise pricing rules. This involves a two-step process:

> First, the *government* specifies the objectives of the enterprise and the constraints. For example, it decides on the target rate of return on capital that has to be achieved by the industry and the magnitude of the state subsidy (if any).

> Second, the *enterprise* determines its pricing policy so as to maximize its objective function subject to the constraints. (p. 459–460)

This two-step decision process is analogous to the Ramsey pricing mechanism but with notable differences. In the Ramsey setting, the constraint (i.e., the amount of tax revenue to be collected) is exogenous, while Atkinson and Stiglitz consider endogenous constraints. For instance, a government setting the required rate of return for one nationalized industry must simultaneously consider the requirements of another industry.

After presenting results on optimal public pricing under constraints, the authors discuss input choice by public enterprises and production efficiency, referencing Boiteux (1956) and the seminal work of Diamond and Mirrlees (1971a, 1971b). This theory concludes that in an economy without pure profits, and for an individualistic social welfare function where at least one good increases utility for all individuals, production efficiency is desirable. This implies transfer prices within the public sector should be marginal costs, but this is not necessarily true for sales to the private sector.

The discussion extends to rules for the shadow price of capital (i.e., the social discount rate) and the use of international prices for open economies as shadow prices by the private sector, viewing these as issues arising in second-best economies. In 'Lecture 16', the authors raise several pertinent questions:

> How do we characterize those goods that are, or ought to be, provided publicly? If the government knew the preferences of all members of the society, how should the supply of each of the public goods be determined? How are the supplies of public goods in fact determined, and how does this contrast with optimal provision? How can the government ascertain the preferences of the members of the society regarding the provision of public goods?

Current mainstream views on SOEs still address these questions but often overlook the theoretical assumptions framing them. For example, Putniņš (2020) summarizes earlier literature suggesting a screening approach using five criteria:

1. Is there a substantial market failure (monopolies or lack of competition, externalities, public goods)? If the answer is 'no', production should be left to the free market. If the answer is 'yes' there is a potential role for an SOE, but conditional on the answer to other questions.
2. Can the market failure be resolved by regulation or targeted taxes/subsidies? If the answer is 'yes', there is no need to establish an SOE.
3. If regulation or tax policies are not feasible, is it possible to specify quality and quantity of the good to be provided through an appropriate contractual arrangement? If the answer is 'yes', public provision through public procurement and private supply is better than public production. Thus, there is no need for an SOE.

4. Under direct public provision through production, SOEs are 'better suited to situations in which there exists an economic market for the outputs, the goals of the government intervention are relatively simple, a relatively large emphasis is placed on financial objectives relative to non-financial ones, and there is the need to be innovative'.
5. Finally, SOEs should not be implemented if the 'welfare losses from government failure, rent seeking, and government intervention induced technical/allocative inefficiency exceed the welfare losses due to the market failure'.

Putniņš (2020, p. 217) frames his approach in terms of Kaldor–Hicks efficiency, where an action that increases social welfare but makes some people worse off can be turned into a Pareto improvement by compensating the losers.

However, comparing social welfare changes 'with' and 'without' an SOE cannot rely on market signals to calculate social benefits and costs, as such markets either lead to undesirable equilibria or do not exist. Thus, framing the reasoning in terms of 'local' market failures can be misleading.

The notion of social efficiency in public economics, as seen in Atkinson and Stiglitz (1980), involves defining social marginal costs, shadow prices, and a social discount rate as policy evaluation criteria. However, most empirical literature on SOEs (and privatizations), including performance analyses reviewed in Section 3, often uses market prices as evaluation signals, referencing 'local' market failures. Since any legal entity under government control is defined as an SOE according to the OECD (2024) definition, there is a risk of evaluating diverse organizations using a benchmark suited only for private or profit-oriented entities. Therefore, we present a benchmark analytical framework more suitable for SOEs under our normative definition.

2.3 A Cost–Benefit Analysis Perspective: Observed vs Shadow Prices

The creation and operation of an SOE can be considered a public investment, thus evaluated in terms of societal welfare changes. Here, we present a simple social cost–benefit analysis (CBA) framework in a second-best environment (Lipsey 2007), as a benchmark model for public policy or project evaluation. We gradually relax some assumptions and discuss issues such as non-benevolent governments, principal–agent problems, state capture, and administrative inefficiency or corruption (Hellman et al. 2003).

Starting with a simple second-best environment: a benevolent, fully informed government aims to maximize social welfare but cannot apply optimal personalized lump-sum taxes. It controls the economy through prices, distortive taxes, quantity constraints on private production and consumption, and property rights laws. Some goods, unprofitable at market prices, may be socially desirable, warranting public production. Public production plans can be executed by SOEs, but they would be costly to delegate to private enterprises, such as through compensatory subsidies or rents.

Government decisions and SOE plans should use shadow prices for inputs and outputs. Shadow prices, the marginal social value of goods, can differ significantly from market prices (Johansson and Kriström 2018; Florio and Pancotti 2023). Establishing an SOE is worthwhile if social benefits exceed social costs at shadow prices compared to alternatives, creating a shadow profit from production.

Unlike socialist planning, the government uses signals like taxes and production plans in a mixed economy. A policy links changes in public sector production plans to signals (Drèze and Stern 1990). For example, providing more carbon-free electricity requires excess demand, net of private provision at tax/subsidy-inclusive market prices. The shadow price of carbon-free electricity relates to the policy enabling this production. Only with the 'right' policy are the shadow prices guiding SOE decisions 'right' (Box 2).

An SOE without a valuable public production plan and supporting right policy is meaningless in social welfare terms. A benevolent and fully informed government needs a supporting policy for an SOE to be necessary but not sufficient. Del Bo and Florio (2012) suggest these conditions for SOEs: (1) private enterprises are free to exit unprofitable markets; (2) the government is benevolent, fully informed, and able to select optimal policies, but cannot use lump-sum taxes or optimal quantity constraints on all goods; (3) public projects pass a social cost–benefit test at shadow prices; (4) public procurement or subsidies to private enterprises are costlier than establishing an SOE.

These conditions justify SOEs as public sector production units filling demand gaps and SOEs are needed when public provision is more efficient than subsidizing private firms, such as in regulated electricity markets (Florio 2013) or drug markets (Florio et al. 2023).

Privatization literature often assumes government inefficiency in managing SOEs while regulators can manage private enterprises efficiently. This dichotomy is flawed. Evaluating economic decisions in welfare terms requires optimal supporting policies across government branches. Suboptimal policies disrupt welfare calculations for public provision/production benefits.

However, these conditions are restrictive. What if the government is not benevolent? This concern will be addressed next.

> **BOX 2 SHADOW PRICES, PUBLIC POLICIES, AND A CBA TEST FOR AN SOE PROJECT**
>
> In an economy with private enterprises and SOEs, a *signal* (s) is any variable that influences private agents' behaviour: $s = (\ldots, s_k, \ldots)$, including producer prices, taxes, rationing, etc. Aggregate net demands are $E = E(s)$; p are producer prices q are consumer prices. Government's social welfare function (SWF): *V(s)* in terms of indirect utilities embodies all the objectives of the government. *Production plans of an SOE* are $z = (\ldots, z_i, \ldots)$. A marginal production change by an SOE is dz. Policy is a rule (ϕ) that associates a state of the economy with SOEs' production plans. The *scarcity constraint* is a system: $E(s) - z = 0$. The social planner's problem is about finding s^* as a solution of: $\max_{(s)} V(s)$ s.t. $E(s) - z = 0$.
>
> A feasible policy is a function $s = \phi(z)$. It associates a public sector production plan z with a vector of signals, such that the scarcity constraints are met. Once such a policy is specified, social welfare is a function of z: $V = V[\phi(z)]$. Shadow prices v are defined as the impact on V of a small change in the SOE provision of a good, given an *optimal supporting policy*. Hence: $v_i = \frac{\partial V}{\partial s} \frac{\partial \phi}{\partial z_i} \forall i = 1, \ldots, I$.
>
> The SOE's project dz is to be accepted if $dV > 0$, i.e., if there is a welfare improvement. This is the cost–benefit analysis (CBA) test: $vdz_i > 0$, welfare increases when inputs/costs (labour, materials) and outputs/benefits (passengers' travel time, etc.) are evaluated at shadow prices v, and net benefits (shadow profits) are positive. An SOE may incur losses at observed prices, but not at shadow prices. Losses are covered by optimal taxation as part of the endogenous solution in terms of signals. If $s = \phi(z)$ is suboptimal, shadow prices are no more leading to the right CBA test for the SOE's plans.
>
> Source: The authors, adapted from Drèze and Stern (1990) and Florio and Pancotti (2023).

2.4 Departures From Second Best: The Quality of Government

The previous discussion should be considered as a benchmark case. Governments consist of individuals with varying degrees of public ethos, motivation, skills, and access to information. To what extent would the previous conditions justifying an SOE withstand the criticism that government failures may be as important as, or even greater than, market failures?

Ignoring for a while the issue of imperfect or asymmetric information, it is useful to distinguish (Hellman et al. 2003; Alesina and Tabellini 2004) between two concepts of non-benevolent government: 'state capture' and 'administrative corruption'. State capture refers to corruption aimed at changing the laws, while administrative corruption refers to corruption aimed at influencing the implementation of existing laws. To simplify, let us assume that any government consists of three types of agents: policy makers, who select the laws (policy options); civil servants or public administrators, who select production plans; and managers of SOEs, who implement the production plans with a degree of discretion. Besley (2006) focuses on good versus bad politicians in terms of political agency in a democracy, while Niskanen (1971) and others focus on a self-interested bureaucracy with a private agenda. Managers of SOEs may be considered similar to bureaucrats according to this public choice literature, as agents ultimately responding to politicians.

We shall now remove the assumptions of the previous second-best world one at a time, and still assume that politicians as principals are benevolent and fully informed, while the agents in the departments and in the public enterprises are self-interested and possibly corrupted. A simple thought experiment in this context suggests that the marginal social value of goods is not affected: civil servants and SOE managers, even if able to distort the production plans, should still be instructed to evaluate projects, that is, marginal changes of the plan, as explained earlier. Shadow prices depend upon optimal policies, not upon optimal plans, because shadow prices by definition concern marginal changes and are not influenced by inframarginal values. Optimal plans are desirable, but if suboptimal plans are adopted, the evaluation of benefits and costs is still possible. The production plan must be feasible, and resources must be available. The plan should respect exogenous constraints, such as the quantity and quality of the labour force to be hired. However, if the social benefits of a (small) project exceed the costs at the 'right' shadow prices, the project would, in principle, increase social welfare (shadow profits), even if the production plan was initially exaggerated or otherwise distorted. In a sense, this is a 'local' government failure, and remedies can be found after monitoring and evaluating the bad implementation of the project in social welfare terms.

The situation is different if self-interested politicians adopt suboptimal policies favourable to themselves or their cronies. This will undermine project selection because shadow prices will not lead decisions in the right (social welfare-enhancing) direction anymore. If voters cannot discriminate between good and bad politicians, according to the political agency theory by Besley (2006), there are three main wide consequences: (1) government fails when policies result in a society being inside its Pareto frontier (Besley 2006, p. 49), meaning there are feasible and more socially desirable policies not adopted; (2b) politicians adopt policies favouring political elites or special interests, with adverse distributional effects, an issue prominent in Pareto's views in his *Treatise of Sociology* (1916), but not in his *Cours d'Économie politique* (1896); (3) politicians adopt policies not leading to a Pareto improvement (in the economist's meaning) compared to a 'do nothing option'.

Let us reverse the previous setting: civil servants and public enterprise managers are benevolent in designing and implementing production plans, while politicians are corrupt. For example, if elected law-makers adopt a tax structure falling under one of the three aforementioned cases, it would always be possible to improve social welfare by not implementing the project and simply improving the tax structure. From the administrator's or manager's perspective, the existing suboptimal policy cannot be ignored because any new SOE's expenditure will create unnecessary welfare losses.

This has the unavoidable consequence that government corruption distorts both decisions to create (e.g., nationalizations) or privatize SOEs. Laffont (2005) suggested that benevolent or very corrupt governments may both privatize (or nationalize) SOEs, for very different reasons. Governments with an intermediate level of corruption may behave by combining two objectives: maximization of social welfare and maximization of private benefits of the politicians, and the outcome in social welfare terms should be evaluated on a case-by-case basis.

In his own words:

> Privatization may happen when they should not because of corruption. The well-documented fact that efficiency increases with privatization should not make us forget that untaxed profits increase even more ... (this is) the necessary price to buy corrupt principals. Sometimes this price is worth it because social welfare also increases. At other times it is not. (Laffont 2005, p. 85)

See Box 3 for illustrative examples of cases in which an SOE should or should not be privatized, or vice versa.

Now, consider an intermediate case: managers of public enterprises, public administrators, and politicians are, to a certain extent, self-interested. However, constitutional arrangements, such as the rule of law and an independent judiciary, establish a system of checks and balances. In such an environment, extracting private rents through policy design and/or mismanagement is relatively costly for both principals and agents. In this context, shadow prices remain sufficient statistics for the value of changes of the public plan. Therefore, investment decisions by SOEs can still be based on welfare-improving reasoning.

An undistorted policy adoption process does not require that all politicians are fully altruistic. This would be unrealistic and an overly strict condition, implying that SOE managers should be instructed to achieve the maximum

> BOX 3 AN SOE UNDER POLITICIANS AND MANAGERS WITH PRIVATE AGENDAS
>
> Consider a monopolistic SOE producing at price = 0 a normalized quantity = 1 of good with social value S; cost C is linearly dependent upon an adverse binary ('high' with probability π, 'low' $(1-\pi)$) selection parameter β and cost-reducing effort, hence: $C = \beta - e$. Disutility of effort is $\psi(e)$. The information is known to the SOE managers, but not to the politicians who appoint them. Managers want to earn rents. Governments reimburse any loss observed ex-post by $C+t$, where t is an incentive to control costs. The social cost is $(C+t)(1+\lambda)$, where $\lambda > 0$ is the marginal cost of public funds because of excess burden of taxation. Hence, if government is benevolent, the net consumer surplus is $V = S - (C+t)(1+\lambda)$; the benefit for the SOE manager is $U = t - \psi(e)$, and social welfare of establishing the SOE is the sum $V + U$: $W = S - (1+\lambda)(\beta - e + \psi(e)) - \lambda U$. This shows that in fact U is a social cost. Suppose now that politicians as well want to extract a private rent b from the SOE. This has an extra cost a for the SOE; and δ is the normalized weight of the politicians' utility, where $\delta = 1$ for a Bentham SWF, and $\delta > 1$ for extra weight given to politicians' utility, so that the SWF is now: $Wc = \delta b + S - (1+\lambda)(\beta - e + b + a + \psi(e)) - \lambda U$.
>
> Laffont (2005) shows that maximization of Wc under a participation constraint such that $U > 0$, determines $b > 0$ if $\delta > 1 + \lambda$. This implies that both politicians and managers now extract rents from the SOE. Managerial rents can be limited by revelation mechanisms in the tradition of Laffont and Tirole (1993), with a menu of contracts defined by t and C corresponding to the b values. Alternatively, by privatization and the appointment of regulatory and auditing mechanisms. Laffont (2005) concludes that politicians with a private agenda will privatize the SOE, and renounce b, only if the transaction is convenient to them compared with the continued SOE. Examples with different model specifications suggest that privatization may or may not be convenient for the society as a whole, the latter particularly is the case when the rents left to the private owners of the former SOE are greater than $(b + a)$.
>
> Source: The authors, adapted from Laffont (2005) and Florio (2006).

possible social welfare. Reasonably good policies can still be adopted if politicians, even if not fully benevolent, are able to extract rents from their office through non-law-making channels. Politicians, especially those in majority rather than opposition parties, can enjoy rents in the form of remuneration, free flights, and accommodation, secretarial staff, and other perks. They benefit from their prestige and high social status and may even enjoy the stamina of political competition per se. However, such forms of selfish motivations do not necessarily imply adopting the 'wrong' policies, where 'wrong' implies deliberately deviating from what can be achieved in social welfare terms, given the available resources, information, and legal, and cultural constraints. Politicians may still adopt welfare-improving policies while enjoying their privileges.

Political agency theory discusses issues relevant to our topic. An example is logrolling activities, described as Coasian political coalitions by Besley (2006). Such coalitions, where votes are exchanged to obtain electoral majority, can be either beneficial or highly damaging in terms of social welfare in an elected parliament. Autocratic systems are prone to government capture, but democracies are not entirely protected from opportunism. Early public choice economists have often focused on rules ('constitutions', 'budgetary rules', etc.) that constrain policy adoption. The welfare effect of such rules cannot be established once and for all. More generally, transparency, freedom of information, tenure duration, public ethos, etc., can be seen as mechanisms to protect policymaking from rent seeking.

2.5 Soft-Budget Constraints

Earlier literature on SOEs was particularly concerned with Kornai's (1979) argument that loss-making firms in the public sector are not disciplined by the same budget constraints that private firms must face. According to Maskin (1996), there are three possible origins of a situation where 'a funding source finds it impossible to keep an enterprise to a fixed budget, i.e., ... the enterprise can extract ex-post a bigger subsidy or loan than would have been considered efficient ex-ante':

1. *Centralized credit*: Suppose there are two types of projects, ex-ante 'slow' and 'fast' in terms of payback. Credit centralization is inefficient because a single bank will fund both, as it cannot discriminate ex-ante, and slow projects anticipate that the bank will not stop funding them ex-post.
2. *Monopoly*: Government bargains investment with a monopolist and offers a subsidy to unprofitable projects. This can be used by the monopolist to extract rents from the government, creating allocative inefficiency, and the social cost of distortionary taxation to fund the subsidy.
3. *Ownership*: Under 'socialism', the banks and firms are jointly owned, leading to inefficiency even under decentralization, as financing decisions are influenced by the firms.

While these models often explained the inefficiency of Soviet-type firms, they have also been used to criticize SOEs in market economies receiving government subsidies or excessive loans. This inspired EU legislation forbidding 'state aid' to firms, with exceptions granted by the European Commission in specific cases as a commitment mechanism.

Empirical evidence does not strongly support the application of soft-budget constraints to contemporary SOEs in developed market economies. First, they are often subject to similar legal constraints as private firms, and second, in regulated industries, regulators often oppose government budgets supporting incumbents. This mostly empirical issue now includes theoretical arguments that depart from Kornai's views. Dewatripont and Maskin (1995), and Bai and Wang (2022) suggest that constraining an agent to immediately terminate a bad project is efficient even with agency issues in project selection. They assume the existence of a project screening agent hired by the principal. The agent's effort is not observable by the principal. Only after the agent implements a selected project does the principal observe its quality and decide to discontinue it. Restricting project termination can decrease the principal's cost by incentivizing the agent to put more effort into initial selection. In the authors' words: 'Although continuing a bad project has a cost to the principal, it is worthwhile as long as the marginal benefit of higher effort is greater than the cost'.

Whether this argument is relevant for SOEs in developed market economies, the cost–benefit analysis discussed previously needs modification when there is information asymmetry and a principal–agent problem involving government departments and SOE managers.

2.6 Information Asymmetry, SOEs, and Public Procurement

Information asymmetry and/or incompleteness have been core topics in public economics for decades, impacting SOE theory. Public provision through public enterprises and public procurement through privately owned enterprises cannot be assumed to bring the same benefits, as outlined by Laffont and Tirole (1993). Under information asymmetry, an SOE may be a socially desirable mechanism to counteract socially costly rents of more efficient agent types. The difficulty in specifying ex-ante contracts is solved by ownership rights, applicable to both private and public enterprises under contract. For example, ownership of a firm includes the right of the shareholder to be continuously informed and may be embodied in the right to appoint directors.

Under asymmetric and incomplete information, public production by SOEs and public procurement by private enterprises will not be welfare equivalent. Public ownership may be superior when the cost of incentivizing the private firm under a procurement contract is too high. Two inefficiencies need to be compared: the socially costly rents earned under public procurement by private owners and the socially costly rents of the not fully benevolent regulator (see Willner 2010 and Ceriani and Florio 2011). Ceriani and Florio (2011) consider a network industry. Initially, the service is provided by a public monopolist with some x-inefficiency compared to cost minimization. Consumer surplus is then computed in a comparative static framework, and indifference conditions are found under an unregulated private monopoly, a regulated private monopoly, a vertically disintegrated monopoly, a duopoly, and a liberalized market. The welfare results depend on the relative size of the x-inefficiencies of the public monopolist, allocative inefficiencies of the private monopoly, the cost of unbundling, and the costs related to establishing a competitive market.

While consumer surplus may be informative and easy to estimate, the comparison of the welfare impact of these inefficiencies cannot be done at market prices because such prices are distorted. This has implications when interpreting empirical analyses comparing profitability between SOEs and private companies, a topic discussed in Section 3.

2.7 Mixed Oligopoly

Private enterprises and SOEs increasingly operate in the same market environment. An important strand of literature related to our topic deals with mixed oligopoly, where a social welfare-maximizing SOE competes in a market with profit-maximizing firms. The message from these models is that the resulting equilibria are often (but not always) welfare-superior to an oligopoly with only private competitors (see De Fraja and Del Bono 1990). Strategic interactions are studied in seminal papers such as those by De Fraja and Del Bono (1990) and Matsumura (1998). More applied perspectives investigate how universal service obligations in certain industries have redefined the role of public enterprises in markets open to competition (see, for example, Bel and Calzada 2009).

Other studies in this context depart from the assumption that public managers have no private agendas and combine mixed oligopoly with public choice issues. A theoretical contribution that combines profit and size or scale objectives is Sappington and Sidak (2003), who opened the way to literature on predatory pricing by SOEs below marginal costs to acquire larger market shares and bigger volumes of operations. In some models, the SOE has an objective function that combines (with a set of weights) social welfare and certain firms' profits or other benefits (Matsumura 1998, Lee et al. 2003, Hindriks and Claude 2006). In others, the scale of operations takes the place of social welfare.

State-Owned Enterprises in Developed Market Economies   19

For a review of the topic, readers are referred to another Cambridge Element in this series: Poyago-Theotoky (2024). In her words:

> The rationale for having a public firm operate along private profit-maximizing firms, is based on the perception that a public firm, by way of its objective to improve social welfare, can act as a regulatory instrument and as such correct, or alleviate at least, market failures associated with imperfect or distorted competition. Exploring whether indeed a public firm can be effective in this, has been a common theme in the theoretical literature on mixed oligopoly. Associated issues relate to privatization or partial-privatization of public firms or the opposite, i.e., nationalization or creation of new public firms, the optimal extent of government participation in these and so on.

The author identifies three topics that are particularly important in recent developments of the literature:

1. Whether the presence of public ownership in an oligopolistic market may have a positive impact on service quality in sectors such as health services, education, transport, and postal services.
2. The potential role of SOEs in these markets in sustaining environmental policy objectives and corporate social responsibility.
3. The different motivations of management and staff when SOEs compete with private firms.

She also reports advancements in the literature on R&D investment under mixed oligopoly, a topic we discuss later from a CBA perspective. An interesting topic within an industrial organization framework is optimal privatization when there are knowledge spillovers, following Gil-Moltó et al. (2011, 2020). The market structures considered in these models are both duopoly and oligopoly, with the usual assumption that the private firm maximizes profits while the SOE maximizes social welfare, both being recipients of R&D subsidies. It has been found that the greater the spillovers, the greater the socially optimal R&D; thus, privatization may decrease aggregate R&D and social welfare. However, if in a mixed market the number of competitors is high, the result can be reversed, and privatization can be beneficial. This suggests that R&D subsidies (including tax expenditures) should be designed by carefully considering market structures.

Readers are referred to Poyago-Theotoky (2024) for details on these models and policy implications. We shall briefly discuss these issues below and in the review of the empirical literature in Section 3.

2.8 Prosocial Behaviour

A substantial stream of more recent literature has explored the role of intrinsic motivation and prosocial behaviour in the public sector, both with theoretical models and some empirical studies (Polidori and Teobaldelli 2013). While this literature has not been systematically linked to SOEs, we believe that this is potentially an interesting research area for our subject given our broader definition (which would include, for example, providers of health and education services). How should SOE theory be redefined when managers and staff are hired from the more altruistic segment of the population, characterized by a distribution of different types with respect to the degree of altruism?

According to Francois and Vlassopoulos (2008), staff with intrinsic motivation may represent an advantage for public organizations, relative to their private counterparts, in terms of level of effort, loyalty to the public mission, and internalization of norms and objectives. The existence of a specific public service motivation is well-known among scholars in public administration. Economists have been slower to consider that some people are happy to contribute to the public good (in a broader meaning, such as public health) and what this implies for the organizations hiring these workers. The empirical evidence suggests that there is a sorting mechanism, with individuals with higher intrinsic motivation for specific jobs being more often hired in public sector organizations. The evidence is not without some controversies, possibly due to confounding factors, but also to the fuzzy boundaries of the concept. Bénabou and Tirole (2006), for example, argue that prosocial behaviour may be driven by three different mechanisms: intrinsic (psychological); extrinsic (material rewards outside the organization); and reputational (which may grant higher rewards elsewhere). This discussion is also related to different concepts of altruism, as illustrated by the idea of 'warm glow' (a form of utility), see Andreoni (1990), Tonin and Vlassopoulos (2010).

Theoretical models, according to Polidori and Teobaldelli (2013), often boil down to agents' utility functions where the ingredients are the satisfaction arising from income-based consumption, less disutility of effort, plus the utility from intrinsic motivation. Impure altruism (Besley and Gathak 2005) would link the latter to effort, while pure altruism (Francois 2000) to the actual level of the public good provided. These models are often framed in a principal–agent relation with different types and moral hazard.

Some of this literature points to the displacing effect on intrinsic motivation of offering monetary reward for effort in the public sector, and ultimately on the inefficiency of public organizations trying to mimic the incentives offered to employees by private companies. Differently from some versions of the 'new public management' approach (Hood 1995), paying more money to do more may have an adverse effect in an organization where doing more (e.g., for patients) or achieving more (e.g., for public health) is seen by the altruistic types as a reward in itself. A theoretical example of why this may happen is Grönblom and Willner (2014), in a model where motivation crowding out can happen in SOEs with performance-related pay, but also in privatized firms. The authors combine agency theory and potential intrinsic motivation and show how 'fat cat' salaries may arise from privatization. They conclude that 'no form of ownership or market structure is always superior if intrinsic motivation can exist or be crowded out in all organizations'. Willner and Grönblom (2020) extend the theoretical analysis to a comparison between public monopoly and oligopoly with potential intrinsic motivation. Their model is inspired by earlier work by James (2005), who explores the impact of extrinsic remuneration on both performance and intrinsic motivation.

In our welfare framework, the benefit–cost ratio of establishing an SOE would be enhanced if it can be predicted that intrinsically motivated personnel would be attracted to work (with higher effort and lower salary than elsewhere) especially in organizations where profit maximization is not the sole or dominant objective (such as health, education, environmental services, research). Of course, empirical analysis is necessary to confirm whether this hypothesis holds true.

2.9 Looking Forward: New Public Missions and New Types of Public Enterprises

The aforementioned social cost–benefit conceptual framework is potentially helpful when considering new public missions for SOEs, such as their role in knowledge creation. There is empirical evidence that private enterprises, including privatized companies, tend to underinvest in R&D for reasons well explained in the seminal theoretical paper by Romer (1990) and in several other contributions of the endogenous growth literature, both theoretical and empirical (see also Section 2.7 for R&D in mixed oligopoly). For an empirical analysis of the decline of corporate R&D, see Arora et al. (2017, p. 3), who study trends of scientific publications co-signed by researchers affiliated with a company since 1980. They conclude that: 'large firms still value the golden eggs of science (as reflected in patents) but seem to be increasingly unwilling to invest in the golden goose itself (the internal scientific capabilities)'.

The core reason for this decline is related to the existence of a positive externality, such that knowledge acquired by a firm spills over to other firms through different transmission channels, including product and process imitation, mobility of researchers across firms, and information provided by publications and patents. The latter, while on one hand offering a temporary legal monopoly to innovators, on the other hand discloses (or should disclose) information that can be instrumental to the creation of further knowledge. Hence, because private firms cannot entirely protect their investments, they will underinvest compared to what would be socially desirable.

While a popular policy course by governments is to offer subsidies or tax rebates to firms to push their R&D activities and spending (the pharmaceutical industry is a notable example), an alternative is the direct provision of knowledge and knowledge-based products and services by government-sponsored organizations. This may happen in different ways, for example through government funding of research universities or institutes. Moreover, some SOEs may be instructed by the government to sustain their R&D expenditures beyond what a short-term cost minimization objective would justify.

The social cost–benefit analysis of such policies, particularly regarding the potential role of SOEs, presents intriguing challenges in the realm of public investment. This is because, unlike the provision of already existing goods, such as transport or electricity, where marginal social value can theoretically be computed based on existing information, evaluating a project that produces a good of unknown value poses a significant question.

If scientific knowledge is viewed as a public good with initially unknown value, its production could be considered a novel (risky) public service, addressing investment challenges that are unappealing to private investors. Organizations specializing in knowledge creation could thus be regarded as new types of public enterprises. For example, the National Institutes of Health (NIH) is the most important organization for biomedical research in the world under the health department of the federal government of the US. While most of the NIH budget (over 50 billion USD in 2023) is devoted to disbursing research grants (ultimately an indirect subsidy to the pharmaceutical industry), its Intramural Research Program is among the largest biomedical R&D public organizations in the world, with around USD 5 billion per year and about 1,200 principal investigators and 5,000 Postdoctoral Fellows. (See details at https://irp.nih.gov/about-us). In a sense, NIH actually or potentially competes with R&D activities of privately owned drug companies. NASA, the European Space Agency, US National Laboratories, and many government-funded bodies and research infrastructures with autonomous budgets and management increasingly resemble a distinct form of SOE delivering knowledge in specific fields as a novel type of public service (Florio 2019).

Lazzarini et al. (2021) suggest that SOEs are given, by governments, the task to perform risky investments along new technological paths. They build an extended agency model where 'given relatively higher levels of managerial autonomy, SOEs may outperform private-owned enterprises (POEs) in some types of inventive output', particularly in countries with a good quality of government. The empirical results confirm this intuition and are discussed in the next section.

More generally, governments have identified a new set of priorities, including energy transition and climate change, sustainable mobility, science and innovation policy, the digital divide, and needs arising from ageing and migration. Additionally, there is a focus on addressing 'capitalism's good jobs problem' (Rodrik and Stantcheva 2021). Public missions of SOEs and their roles may be reshaped by these policy priorities in countries where governments support a new sustainable development agenda for the twenty-first century. This field is still developing, but government science and innovation policies increasingly invest in large-scale research and technology infrastructures, exemplified by initiatives like the European Strategy Forum on Research Infrastructures (ESFRI). A cost–benefit analysis of public investment in research infrastructure emphasizes forecasting benefits primarily deriving from R&D, including human capital formation, technological spillovers, direct cultural effects, and a public good value as a form of indirect cultural effect, even when the future value of discovery is entirely unknown, see Box 4.

BOX 4 CBA OF RESEARCH INFRASTRUCTURES

For research infrastructures (RIs) the net present value of social benefits can be estimated by a simple equation:

$$NPV_{RI} = [SC + HC + TE + AR + CU] + B_n - [K + L_s + L_o + OP + EXT]$$

Benefits include: SC = knowledge output value; HC = human capital formation; TE = technological externalities to firms supplying technologies; AR = benefits to downstream users of innovations; CU = cultural goods arising from outreach activities; Bn = non-use value based on the willingness to pay of taxpayers for scientific knowledge, a public good. Costs include: K = economic value of capital; Ls = labour cost of scientists; Lo = other staff costs; OP = other operating costs; EXT = negative externalities arising from the construction and operation of the RI. Labour costs are estimated by shadow wages. In general, marginal costs or willingness to pay are proxies of shadow prices. Each component is taken at its present value, the discounting process is $s_t = 1/(1 + r)^t$ where r is the social discount rate. SC is measured by the opportunity cost of scientists to produce a publication and to read and cite another publication. HC is valued as the increased earnings gained by former RI's students and

> Box 4 (cont.)
>
> former employees, since the time they leave the RI project, against a suitable counterfactual scenario. *TE* is given by the discounted incremental shadow profits $S_j s_t \Pi_{jt}$ by companies (j) of the RI's supply chain or by other economic agents who have benefit from a learning externality. *AR* is project specific (health for example), and each of them ultimately is related to the willingness to pay for them by users. *CU* carried out by the RI produce different cultural effects on the general public, which can be valued by estimating the willingness to pay W_{gt} for such activities. Finally, the term B_n captures the social value of a pure public good of discovery of nature by taxpayers and can be proxied by stated or revealed willingness to pay for discovery, similar to non-use values in environmental economics.
>
> Source: Florio (2019).

3 Empirics

We now consider SOEs from an empirical perspective and discuss to what extent the literature in the past twenty years has been able to measure performance of SOEs against the issues raised in our conceptual framework discussion. As we shall see, the empirical literature has tended to rely, for many reasons, on the formalistic definition of SOEs that we have criticized in Section 2.1 and on performance criteria that are not fully consistent with welfare analysis. Aligning theory and empirics of SOEs is still unfinished work. We are now conducting a positive analysis through the lens of normative theory.

We conduct an in-depth exploration of scholarly literature regarding the comparative performance of private and public enterprises in developed countries over the last two decades, where the performance empirical measures are critically discussed from the perspective of applied welfare economics. Moreover, the examination emphasizes how the empirical findings are affected by contextual conditions, institutional factors, and methodological issues. Our review encompasses contributions from the fields of economics and management, occasionally extending into related social sciences. Before delving into the analysis of the literature on the impact of ownership on performance measures, a quick overview of the importance of state ownership is useful.

Worldwide, the importance of SOEs is significant. According to Kwiatkowski et al. (2023), the share of SOEs on the Fortune Global 500 lists[3] from 2005 to

---
[3] These lists include the top world companies by revenues (https://fortune.com/franchise-list-page/global-500-methodology-2023).

2020 substantially increased: in 2005, the SOEs on the Fortune list were only 64, while in 2020, there were 141 SOEs. In the same time span, the share of SOEs doubled in terms of revenues (to almost 30%), more than tripled in assets, and SOE employees doubled. China is the main driver behind this trend, a notable fact that should be discussed in the context of the gargantuan growth and transformation of the Chinese economy and governance. This is, however, beyond the scope of this Element, as our focus is on developed market economies with some broadly similar core governance mechanism, such as the OECD Member States.

Ten years ago, according to the OECD (2014) " ... SOEs in the OECD area are valued at over 2 trillion USD and employ over 6 million people. Although they do not account for a particularly high share of the productive economy (2.5% of national employment on average), SOEs are highly concentrated in strategic sectors on which large parts of the private economy depend. Half of SOEs by value operate in the network industries (telecoms, electricity and gas, transportation, and postal services)."[4]

Since then, the role of SOEs has further increased in the OECD area as well. Despite a widespread privatization wave worldwide, the presence of some form of state ownership in firms is still non-negligible, especially in the aftermath of the 2008 crisis. Recent figures suggest that the share of non-financial SOEs among the largest firms ranges from 2.3% in emerging economies to 4.5% in advanced economies in 2018 (with a value of 13.3% for China). In terms of sectors, SOEs are prevalent in network industries, such as utilities, transportation, and banking (IMF 2020). To have a birds' eye view of the evolution of the extent of state ownership in developed countries in the past twenty years, we provide figures from two sources of information: the OECD Economy Wide Product Market Regulation (PMR) indicators (see Koske et al. 2015) and the dataset described in De Lange and Merlevede (2020).

The OECD *Public Ownership* indicator is a composite measure that reflects information on the scope of SOEs, government involvement in network sectors, direct public control over enterprises, and the governance of SOEs. Information is collected through questionnaires to key actors (ministries, regulators, and other relevant authorities) in different sectors and the final indicator ranges from 0 to 6, with lower values corresponding to less public ownership (Vitale et al. 2020).

Figure 1 represents the *Public Ownership* indicator, for OECD countries, grouped by continent, in the latest year available, 2018. The average value across the sample is slightly above 2, suggesting a modest influence, in terms of de jure regulation, of public ownership. There is however variability across countries, with values around three for Switzerland, France, Poland, and Norway.

---

[4] https://web-archive.oecd.org/fr/2015-12-03/260474-oecd-dataset-size-composition-soe-sectors.htm

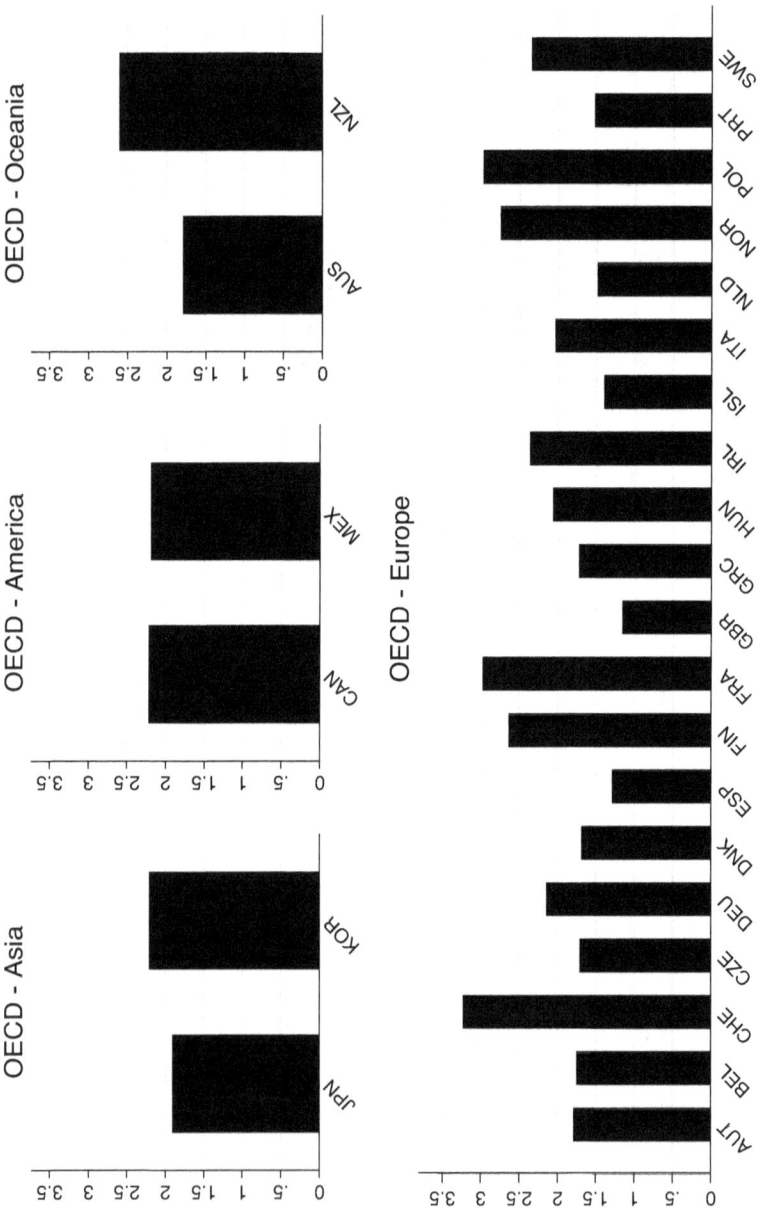

Figure 1 Public ownership, selected countries, 2018.

Source: *OECD Economy wide PMR indicator, authors' elaboration.*

Looking at the evolution over time of the indicator for each country, the situation in Europe is rather heterogeneous. For a set of countries (Austria, Belgium, the Czech Republic, Spain, Finland, France, Greece, Hungary, Italy, the Netherlands, Poland, and Portugal) there is an overall decreasing trend over time in the considered period (1998–2013),[5] while for another set of countries (Denmark, Germany, Ireland, Sweden, Switzerland and the UK), the value increased in 2008, during and after the crisis, possibly reflecting the various forms of state intervention and rescue activity. Looking at the other continents, available data reveal an increasing trend post-2008. Countries with lower levels of public ownership, in response to the 2008 crisis, experienced an increase in public ownership, while European countries, with the exceptions mentioned previously, where values of the indicator were on average higher, continued along the previous decreasing path.

For a similar time period (2002–2010) in Europe, De Lange and Merlevede (2020) collected information on 5,944,109 firms (most of them small enterprises) each year for twenty-seven European countries, and report that, out of these, 21,377 are majority SOEs and 6,681 are minority SOEs (mostly large firms). Therefore, on average, and over the considered time period, SOEs (both minority and majority state-owned) represent 0.5% of all firms, but this figure is not very informative, as the share among major companies is higher. This average yearly figure hides significant time and country variation. As already mentioned, after the 2008 crisis, governments across Europe have increased their direct involvement in firms, in aggregate increasing state ownership in the economy. Figures presented in De Lange and Merlevede (2020) document that the share of majority participations in the twenty-seven European countries, increases on average between 2005 and 2012.

The significant and rising prominence of state ownership in many industries and countries underscores the importance of renewed attention to the performance of enterprises characterized by some form of state ownership, a task we undertake in the subsequent discussion.

When looking at the economic impact of firm ownership, a set of relevant questions would include asking if SOEs are in general more social welfare-enhancing (e.g., in terms of quality and price), empirically more productive, more innovative, more competitive on international markets, and overall more effective in terms of societal impact (e.g., on environmental policy goals) than their private counterparts, after controlling for confounding factors. Ultimately,

---

[5] Unfortunately, a change in the methodology adopted by the OECD does not allow direct comparison between the 2018 data and previous vintages, but a few comments on the evolution of public ownership in OECD countries can be made. Focusing on average values for the 1998–2013 time interval, European countries present the highest value of the indicator for public ownership (2.99), followed by Oceania (2.46), the American continent (2.11) and Asia (1.89).

the answer to this set of performance questions relies on the analysis of empirical evidence. While a vast array of scholars, from both a managerial and economics perspective, have examined this issue by means of case studies, statistical and econometric analyses, they did not reach a strong consensus overall, making it difficult to provide a clear and straightforward answer to the initial questions. On the brighter side, the main findings documented by relevant researchers in the field can be organized around common themes to summarize the evidence on the effect of ownership on a firm's behaviour and results and to highlight aspects that need to be further explored. By the end of this section, the reader will be aware of the common ground on which we stand on in terms of the impact of private or public ownership on firm-level performance, and see the paths which must be more thoroughly explored in the future to better understand this issue.

As detailed below, we have gathered a robust collection of empirical studies, ensuring that our analysis is grounded in the most reputable and relevant scholarly work in the field of SOEs' performance. Initially, to identify the relevant literature, we drew upon our own previous research on SOEs and on privatization. Cumulatively the authors of this Element have published a number of articles and books that in turn cite over one thousand papers and books. Additionally, the Scopus and Web of Science databases were thoroughly searched using specific keywords, aiming to comprehensively integrate empirical literature. In particular, we recurred to search terms such as 'state-owned', 'state-ownership', 'government-controlled', 'state-invested enterprise'.[6] Further refinements have been incorporated by referencing existing surveys (e.g., Megginson and Liu 2022). A few caveats and notes on the scope of the review presented in the following sections are in order. The basis for the analysis is the scholarly, academic literature on the comparative performance of private versus public enterprise exclusively or mainly in developed countries over the past twenty years, in English. Published contributions in economics, management, and occasionally other social sciences are included. The scope, role and functioning of SOEs in developing countries are rather different from the situation in developed countries and is thus not considered here. Similarly, as mentioned in our Introduction, Chinese SOEs are excluded as both the environment and the rules of the game are very country specific and differ significantly from other parts of the world, and available evidence often departs from accepted standards.[7]

We conducted a screening process to focus on a manageable number of articles deemed highly relevant to the topic. This selection was based on the quality and

---

[6] The search strategy has been refined by incorporating additional keywords to identify articles focused on firm performance ('innovation', 'performance', 'impact', 'return*', 'efficien*') and employing an empirical approach ('econometric', 'regression', 'empiric*', 'observ*', 'analys*', 'find*', 'inference', 'panel', 'data', 'investigat*').

[7] For a comprehensive and critical overview of state ownership in China, see Milhaupt (2020).

relevance of the journals where the articles were published, the reputation of the authors in the field, and the number of citations received. The goal of the analysis is research outputs that deal with the comparison, along different dimensions, between firms that differ in terms of ownership. Research focusing on total or partial private and public ownership is considered, while contributions that focus primarily on the effects of privatization are, for the most part, excluded. There is a strand of earlier literature that has extensively examined the before–after effects of the privatization program, initiated in the 1980s in the UK (see, e.g., Florio 2004, Gupta 2005, Boardman et al. 2016). The aim of the present review, however, is neither to add to the discussion on the merits or demerits of privatization nor to discuss the more recent trend pointing towards a slowing down or a reversal of this paradigm (on this issue see, among others, Hefetz and Warner 2004, and Clò et al. 2015). Our interest lies in the effect of type of ownership, if any, on firms' performance under the umbrella of welfare analysis. The interested reader could start from Megginson and Netter (2001), Clifton et al. (2003, 2006), Florio (2004) and Megginson (2016) for an overview of what we have learned on the effects of privatization, albeit with quite different views and conclusions, and with the methodological issue that privatization decisions were often endogenous, hence any before–after comparison is biased by the non-random nature of the process.

As detailed in Table 1 our selection efforts identified a relatively small sample of sixty-one articles (in chronological order), along with some other articles that, due to their specificity, will be discussed separately in the following paragraphs (Tables 2 and 3). The full references that appear in Tables 1, 2 and 3 are marked with an asterisk in the bibliography. Table 1 also provides essential information extracted from these papers, which will serve as the foundation for the discussion in the subsequent paragraphs.

Specifically, the impact of private versus public ownership is analyzed by considering studies that have dealt with different performance measures. We start with the most common performance indicator in the scholarly literature: profitability (with various accounting ratios). This is, for many reasons, a 'bad' performance indicator from a welfare analysis point of view, and we will discuss the results accordingly. More relevant to our normative definition of SOEs are other indicators, including productivity, innovation, environmental sustainability, keeping in mind that the questions arising from the previous sections are often not well captured by the empirical strategies in the literature. We also consider internationalization of SOEs, a strategy that poses other problems in terms of the coherence between a public mission, essential for SOEs in a normative perspective, and 'going abroad'.

We consider factors such as the sample period, geographical area, and the specific industry under scrutiny. This approach allows us to discern whether the

Table 1 Review of the empirical literature on the performance of SOEs

Article	Dependent variable (Performance measure: productivity/ profitability/ innovation/ environment/ other)	Sample period	Geographical area	Industry	Institutional quality, regulation, political factors (Control/moderator/no)	SOE measure (Dichotomous/discrete/continuous)	Estimation method	State-ownership effect (Positive/negative/not significant/mixed)
Dewenter & Malatesta (2001)	Profitability: return on assets (ROA); return on equity (ROE); return on sales (ROS)	1975, 1985, 1995	Cross-country	Cross-industry	No	Dichotomous	Ordinary least squares (OLS)	Negative
Backx et al. (2002)	Profitability: ROS; ROA	1993–1997	World	Airline passenger carriers	Control: degree of competition	Discrete: private, mixed, public	OLS	Negative
Dalen & Gómez-Lobo (2003)	Productivity: total factor productivity (TFP)	1987–1997	Norway	Bus carriers	Control: Regulation	Dichotomous	Cost frontier model	Positive
Kwoka (2005)	Productivity: TFP	1989	USA	Electricity	No	Dichotomous	OLS	Mixed (depends on sub-sector)
Bozec et al. (2006)	Profitability: ROS; ROA Productivity: data envelopment analysis (DEA); technical efficiency; labour productivity growth	1976–2001	Canada	Cross-industry	No	Dichotomous: dummy for privatization	Pooled OLS	Mixed (rejecting major gain from privatizations)
Earnhart & Lizal (2006)	Environment: pollutant emissions	1993–1998	Czech Republic	Cross-industry	No	Dichotomous	Unbalanced panel analysis	Positive (increased state ownership improves environmental performance)
Dal Bo & Rossi (2007)	Other: Labour. Full time employees (firm level)	1994–2001	13 Latin American countries	Electricity	Control: Corruption	Dichotomous	OLS	Negative

Study	Outcome	Period	Country	Sector	Other variables	Ownership	Method	Effect of private ownership
Roy & Yvrande-Billon (2007)	Productivity: TFP	1995–2002	France	Urban public transport	Moderator: Regulation (type of contract/tendering)	Discrete: private, mixed, SOE	SFA	Negative
Asaftei et al. (2008)	Productivity: TFP growth	1995–2003	Romania	Manufacturing	Moderator: Degree of competition	Discrete: private, mixed, SOE	OLS/Heckman selection model	Mixed (depends on competition. In competitive markets, private and privatized firms do better)
Goldeng et al. (2008)	Profitability: ROA; costs/sales	1990–1999	Norway	Cross-industry	Control: competition; governance (management incentives and owner monitoring)	Dichotomous	OLS	Negative
Wolf (2009)	Other: Oil and gas production	1987–2006	Cross-country	Oil industry	No	Dichotomous: three dummy variables (fully state-owned; majority state-owned companies; minority state-owned companies)	Multivariate regression	Negative
Growitsch & Wetzel (2009)	Productivity: physical efficiency (firm level) – freight tonne-km)	2000–2004	Europe	Railways	Control: vertical market integration / separation	Dichotomous	DEA	Positive
Brau et al. (2010)	Prices	1991–2007	EU–15	Gas sector	Control: market structure	Discrete	Panel data models	Positive (lower prices)
Bacchiocchi et al. (2011)	Prices and quality	1997–2003	EU–15	Telecomms	Control: market structure	Discrete	Dynamic estimators for panel data	Positive (lower prices and higher quality)
Eller et al. (2011)	Productivity: TFP	2002–2004	Cross-country	Oil sector	Control: vertical market integration	Continuous	DEA	Negative
Fiorio & Florio (2011)	Customer satisfaction	2000–2002–2004	EU–15	Residential electricity sector	Control: liberalization	Discrete	Latent variable models	Positive
Sterlacchini (2012)	Innovation: R&D expenditure	2000–2007	Developed countries (world)	Electricity generation sector	No	Dichotomous	OLS	Positive
Boitani et al. (2013)	Productivity: TFP	1997–2006	Europe	Urban transport	Moderator: competition for the market-	Discrete: private, mixed, public	OLS	Negative

Table 1 (cont.)

Article	Dependent variable (Performance measure: productivity/ profitability/ innovation / environment/ other)	Sample period	Geographical area	Industry	Institutional quality, regulation, political factors (Control / moderator / no)	SOE measure (Dichotomous / discrete / continuous)	Estimation method	State-ownership effect (Positive / negative / not significant / mixed)
Driffield (2013)	Profitability: ROA Productivity: TFP	1998–2006	Central East Europe		Control: liberalization reforms	Dichotomous	ML estimation	Negative, but liberalization reforms impact (positively) SOEs more
Inoue et al. (2013)	Profitability: ROA; market-to-book	1995–2009	Brazil	Publicly traded firms	Moderator: local institutional quality	Dichotomous	FE Panel regressions	Mixed
Meyer & Pac (2013)	Environment: emissions of pollutants	2004–2009	Eastern Europe	Energy utility	Control: partisan policy variables	Dichotomous	Panel data models, IV	Negative
Scheffler et al. (2013)	Productivity: technical efficiency	2009	Germany	Public bus transport	Control: Regulation (tendering)	Dichotomous	SFA	Not significant
Fiorio & Florio (2013)	Prices	1991–2007	EU–15	Residential electricity sector	Control: market structure	Discrete	Dynamic estimators for panel data	Positive (lower prices)
Coulomb & Sangnier (2014)	Profitability: stock market returns	2007	France		Control: political variables	Continuous	OLS	Not significant
Growitsch & Stronzik (2014)	Prices	1989–2007	Europe	Gas sector	Control: regulation	Discrete	Dynamic estimators for panel data	Positive (lower prices)
Jory & Ngo (2014)	Profitability: stock price; operating performance	1987–2009	USA (acquirers); world (targets)		Moderator: institutional quality	Dichotomous	Logistic regressions	Negative (bidders of SOE fare worse than bidders of non-SOE both in terms of stock price and operating performance)
Le Lannier & Porcher (2014)	Productivity: TFP	2009	France	Water supply	No	Dichotomous	DEA and SFA	Positive
Borisova et al. (2015)	Profitability: cost of debt	1991–2010	Cross-country	Cross-industry	No	Continuous and dichotomous	TWFE model; Heckman two-stage model; 2SLS IV model	Mixed (negative in normal times but positive during financial crises)
Ben-Nasr (2016)	Profitability: firm value	1981–2012	Global	Cross-industry	No	Dichotomous	TWFE	Negative

Study	Dependent variable	Period	Country	Industry	Moderator/Control	Ownership measure	Method	Result
Benito et al. (2016)	Profitability: market value (Tobin's Q); ROA; ROS	2000–2010	No	Cross-industry; publicly listed	No	Continuous (% of equity held by the government)	Random effects (RE) specification with robust standard errors clustered at the company level	Positive (although moderate)
Boardman et al. (2016)	Productivity: approximate TFP	1982–2018	Canada	Cross-industry	No	Dichotomous: dummy for privatized firms and always private firms	Difference-in-differences	Negative
Borghi et al. (2016).	Productivity: TFP	2002–2009	Europe	Electricity	Moderator: institutional quality	Dichotomous	Pooled OLS	Mixed (positive in high-quality institutional environments)
Calza et al. (2016)	Environment: environmental proactivity, proxied by the company's carbon disclosure score, CDS	2012	Germany, Switzerland and Austria, Italy, France, and Spain and Portugal	Cross-industry	Control: regulation (environmental regulatory stringency)	Continuous: percentage of shares held by the state	OLS	Positive
Díaz & Charles (2016)	Productivity: TFP	1995–2010	France	Urban transport	Moderator: regulation of contract design	Discrete: private, mixed, SOE	Panel data (non-parametric and semi-parametric methods)	Mixed (negative for SOEs; positive for mixed)
Estrin et al. (2016)	Other: degree of internationalization	2010	World	Cross-industry	Moderator: Institutional and governance measures	Dichotomous	Propensity Score Matching	Not significant
Beuselinck et al. (2017)	Profitability: firm value (cumulative stock return over the crisis period; market-to-book ratio)	2005–2009	European countries (28)	Cross-industry	Moderator: institutional quality	Continuous and dichotomous	Propensity Score Matching + OLS	Positive (driven by firms in countries with high institutional quality)
Clò et al. (2017a)	Environment: emissions released / carbon intensity	1990–2012	EU27, no, TK	Sample selection: Electricity generation sector	No	Continuous: level of public ownership	TWFE; RE	Positive
Clò et al. (2017b)	Profitability: operating profit margin of the target company in the year before the deal	2005–2012	Global	Cross-industry	No	Dichotomous	OLS at the deal level	Mixed (negative for SOEs; not significant for state invested enterprises)

Table 1 (cont.)

Article	Dependent variable (Performance measure: productivity/ profitability/ innovation/ environment/ other)	Sample period	Geographical area	Industry	Institutional quality, regulation, political factors (Control / moderator / no)	SOE measure (Dichotomous / discrete / continuous)	Estimation method	State-ownership effect (Positive / negative / not significant / mixed)
Del Bo et al. (2017)	Other: multiple characteristics of acquirers in M&A deal	2004–2012	World	Cross-industry	No	Dichotomous	Multinomial logit/OLS	Positive
Karolyi & Liao (2017)	Other: M&A (number of cross-border deals)	1990–2008	Cross-country	Cross-industry	Control: both institutional quality and political factors	Dichotomous	Panel regression	Positive
Suárez-Varela et al. (2017)	Productivity: TFP	2013	Spain	Water services	No	Dichotomous	DEA	Mixed
Szarzec & Nowara (2017)	Profitability: profit margin; ROE; current ratio; solvency ratio	2007–2013	Central-Eastern Europe	Cross-industry	No	Continuous: % of state-owned capital	Mann-Whitney U test	Mixed
Chen et al. (2018)	Other: internationalization (propensity of completion of cross-border acquisitions after public announcement; acquisition size)	2004–2013	Global	Cross-industry	Moderator: Home budget balance risk; ICRG's risk for budget balance index Control: home minority investor protection; home government stability; host rule of law	Continuous: Government blockholding: the total percentage of voting shares of all government blockholders based in the acquirer's home nation	Analysis at the deal level (cross-border acquisitions). Two-step Heckman-style selection model	Mixed (U-Shaped relationship)
Jaslowitzer et al. (2018)	Profitability: Tobin's Q	2097–2013	Europe	Cross-industry	No	Continuous: % of state-ownership to total ownership	Pooled OLS	Negative
Lazzarini & Musacchio (2018)	Profitability: ROA; Tobin's Q	1997–2012	Cross-country (66 countries)	Cross-industry	No	Dichotomous: two dummy variables (majority SOEs, minority SOEs)	difference-in-differences	Not significant
Stiel et al. (2018)	Productivity: TFP	2002–2013	Germany	Electricity	Control: Governance structure	Dichotomous	OLS/ACF (Ackerberg et al. 2015)	Not significant
Bortolotti et al. (2019)	Other: innovativeness (R&D spending and patents)	2000–2009	Europe	Cross-industry	Moderator: financial constraints and electoral variables	Dichotomous with additional controls for majority/minority government owned	OLS and 2SLS	Mixed

Study	Dependent variable	Years	Country	Industry	Moderator/Control	SOE measure	Method	Result
Castelnovo et al. (2019)	Productivity: TFP	2007–2015	World	Telecomms	Moderator: institutional quality	Discrete: private, mixed, SOE	Pooled OLS	Mixed (positive in high-quality institutional environments)
Grøgaard et al. (2019)	Other: internationalization (entry mode of inward foreign direct investment: (1) purchase of stand-alone assets rather than firms; (2) acquired ownership percentage)	2007–2013	Global (but investing in Canada)	Oil & gas industry	Moderator: government quality and market orientation of the home country	Continuous: percentage of shares owned by the home state in the investing unit	Logistic regression analysis and Tobit model	Mixed
del-Rio & de Alegria, I. (2019)	Prices	2003–2013	EU-15	Industrial electricity sector	Control: market structure	Discrete	Dynamic estimators for panel data	Positive (lower prices)
Biggar & Söderberg (2020)	Other: price stability	1998–2007	Sweden	Municipalities with a district heating service	No	Dichotomous	Pooled OLS and IV	Not significant
Clò et al. (2020)	Innovation: firm-level patenting	2007–2015	Cross-country	Telecomms	Yes	Dichotomous	Poisson regression model	Positive
De Lange & Merlevede (2020)	Profitability, productivity, innovation, other (several measures)	2002–2012	Europe	Cross-industry	Moderator: (1) region-specific marketization, i.e. development of market-based mechanisms; (2) dummy for government-'encouraged' industries	Continuous and dichotomous (different definitions of government control)	Pooled OLS	Negative, but contained in countries with better scores on institutional characteristics
Inoue (2020)	Performance: ROS Other: employment	2004–2014	Brazil	Municipal water utilities	Moderator: election years Control: political and local institutional quality variables	Dichotomous	Pooled OLS; difference-in-differences	Negative (higher employment levels and lower financial performance in election years). This effect is mitigated by local institutional quality and political variables

Table 1 (cont.)

Article	Dependent variable (Performance measure: productivity/ profitability/ innovation/ environment/ other)	Sample period	Geographical area	Industry	Institutional quality, regulation, political factors (Control / moderator / no)	SOE measure (Dichotomous / discrete / continuous)	Estimation method	State-ownership effect (Positive / negative / not significant / mixed)
Kabaciński et al. (2020)	Performance: ROA; EBIT; current ratio; operational efficiency	2013–2015	Poland	Cross-sector	No	Dichotomous	Discriminant analysis	Mixed (depending on the performance variable)
Kalasin (2020)	Other: international expansion (number of host countries in which firms set up foreign subsidiaries)	2003–2008	Emerging markets	Cross-sector	No	Continuous: ratio of state-ownership to total ownership	Negative binomial regression	Mixed
Qingyuan et al. (2020)	Other: level of investments (yearly growth in capital expenditure)	2001–2015	Europe	Cross-sector	Moderator: election years	Dichotomous	Seemingly unrelated regression	Positive (increase in corporate investments in election years)
Aguilera et al. (2021)	Performance and productivity (several measures)	53 years	Cross-country	Cross-sector	Moderator: both institutional quality and political factors	Continuous and DICHOTOMOUS	Meta-analytic regression analysis	Mixed
Lazzarini et al. (2021)	Innovation: firm-level patenting	1997–2012	Cross-country	Cross-sector	Yes	Dichotomous	Pooled OLS	Positive
Castelnovo (2022)	Innovation: firm-level patenting	2011–2018	Europe	Cross-sector	No	Dichotomous	Negative binomial regression	Positive
Calzada and Díaz-Serrano (2023)	Prices	1995–2009	EU-15	Telecomms	Control: market structure	Discrete	Dynamic estimators for panel data	Not significant

effects of public ownership on performance, as identified in empirical literature, exhibit any discernible temporal trends and how they vary across different market structures. A set of conditioning factors in explaining this relationship are considered, namely institutional quality, political factors, and corporate governance. Furthermore, the comprehensiveness of the dichotomous variable distinguishing private and SOEs is discussed, with a brief overview of hybrid organizations. Finally, we scrutinize the diverse empirical methods employed in existing analyses. By doing so, we aim to delineate which empirical approaches have predominated thus far, how they might have shaped the empirical evidence obtained to date, and which recent econometric advancements could prove instrumental in defining and guiding the future trajectory of this research field.

It is important to note that our selection exclusively concerns papers with an explicit empirical/quantitative angle, and that were published in the last two decades. However, within the text, we will also reference articles of a more qualitative nature that remain relevant to the current analysis. Finally, we exclude banks and other financial actors in the review, and we refer the interested reader to specialized contributions (i.e., Cornett et al. 2010, Lazzarini et al. 2015, Eslava and Freixas 2021).

In the subsequent paragraphs, we will delve deeper into each of the aforementioned aspects, providing a comprehensive exploration of the key elements that have been succinctly summarized in Table 1.

3.1 Performance: What is Measured and What Should be?

A significant portion of empirical literature on the state-ownership effect on performance refers to a rather standardized regression model, at least in its baseline form (see Box 5). What distinguishes the existing literature, however, is how firm-level performance is measured. A first set of measures broadly considers a firm as successful by looking at its ability to generate profits. Profitability can then be measured by looking at simple measures of profits or profit growth, or by resorting to a series of accounting measures, usually in the form of ratios. Empirical studies comparing private and public enterprises along these lines are discussed in Section 3.1.1.

Performance can be measured from another angle by considering a firm's ability to combine inputs in an efficient manner in order to produce the maximum amount of output, given the technological possibilities available to the firm, summarized by the production function. This type of reasoning leads to the use of productivity measures, the simplest being input productivity, most notably labour, or total factor productivity when all inputs are considered (Section 3.1.2).

Typically, these two families of indicators are usually deemed sufficient to analyze and compare privately owned firms. However, when considering SOEs,

BOX 5 COMPARING THE PERFORMANCE OF SOEs AND POEs

Most of the analyses proposed in the empirical literature to compare the performance of SOEs and POEs are based on a model, more or less explicitly formalized, of the following type:

$$Y_i = \alpha + \beta SOE_i + \sum_{j=1}^{J} \gamma_j Z_{ij} + \sum_{c=1}^{C} \delta_c W_{ic} + \sum_{s=1}^{S} \eta_s V_{is} + \varepsilon_i \quad (1)$$

where:

- the observation unit i is an individual firm;
- the dependent variable Y_i is the performance variable of interest;
- SOE_i is the explanatory variable of interest, identifying SOEs alternatively through dichotomous or continuous measures;
- Z_{ij} are firm-level control variables, where j = 1, ..., J;
- W_{ic} are country level control variables, where c = 1, ..., C;
- V_{is} are industry level control variables, where s = 1, ..., S;
- ε_i represents the error term.

In this model, the coefficient β represents the *state-ownership effect* on firm-level performance. When panel data are available, the temporal dimension t can be exploited by including time fixed effects, f_t, and time-variant controls (Z_{ijt}, W_{ict}, V_{ist}).

By including control variables at each level, the baseline model allows for specific influences of firm, country, and industry characteristics on the dependent variable. However, many papers circumscribe the scope of analysis by narrowing the sample of observation to a single country (or geographic area) or to a specific industry (or group of industries). This has the benefit of comparing SOEs and POEs within a more homogenous firms' domain, albeit at the inevitable cost of reduced generalizability.

The broader and more heterogeneous the sample of considered firms, the more relevant the endogeneity concerns associated with the fact that the state does not randomly select firms in which to hold ownership stakes. In this case, to better identify the *treatment effect* of state ownership, it can be useful to employ matching methods that make the *treated* group (SOEs) and the *control* group of POEs as comparable as possible, except for ownership differences. This involves adopting matching techniques suitable for selecting a subset of POEs that resemble SOEs based on a specific set of observables. See, for example, Abadie et al. (2004) and Abadie and Imbens (2011) for details on nearest-neighbour matching estimators. At

> Box 5 (cont.)
>
> the researcher's discretion, the search for similar firms can be conducted by country or by industry to impose matching within a sufficiently homogeneous environment.
>
> Source: The authors, adapted from the referenced empirical literature in this section.

additional aspects should be taken into account. When comparing private and public enterprises, one should bear in mind that SOEs might have a broader mandate than their private counterparts and be assigned, by their government principals, multiple objectives, other than simple profit maximization or productive efficiency. Therefore, other measures of performance should be considered and more research is still needed to reach a consensus on how to translate the multiple goals that characterize SOEs into testable hypotheses.

3.1.1 Profitability Indicators

Firms are usually thought of as profit-maximizing entities (see Section 2.1). Thus, in this perspective, a natural benchmark for comparing private firms and SOEs is examining whether ownership has an effect on profitability indicators, with the caveat that a firm can be highly profitable for the 'wrong reasons' and in fact part of the reported profits can be considered as rents in an economic perspective. Unfortunately, accounting indicators do not convey the difference, and are taken at face value by most of the empirical literature that we discuss later.

A few of the most well-known and used indicators include Return on Sales (ROS), Return on Assets (ROA) and Return on Equity (ROE) and Tobin's q, the latter two for listed firms. ROS is typically used to evaluate a firm's operational efficiency and provides information on how much of total sales are actually converted into profits. It is computed as profits over sales. ROA summarizes how much profit a firm generates by means of its assets, and thus hints towards the efficiency of a firm's management structure in generating value for investors from the economic resources it has invested in the past. It is computed as profits over total assets. ROE is an indicator of a firm's ability to generate profits from shareholders' investments. It is computed as profits over shareholder equity (or market value). Tobin's q sheds light on a firm's equilibrium between market and intrinsic value. It is computed as a firm's market value divided by its assets' replacement cost.

Studies based on the analysis of samples of large and in some cases listed firms, from different non-financial sectors and with an international coverage are the main focus of this subsection. Presented in a chronological order, the first contributions, such as Dewenter and Malatesta (2001), find that state ownership is associated with lower profitability, while more recent papers find that SOEs are similar, or even better performing, than POEs. Single country studies, of which we present a selection based on geographic coverage, present a similar time trend, with earlier studies suggesting that SOEs are not as performing as POEs; however, results might be dependent on the specific country analyzed.

Dewenter and Malatesta (2001) offer a seminal and thorough analysis of the relative performance of private versus public enterprises in financial terms. With data for 1975, 1985, and 1995 for the 500 Fortune companies, the authors consider the impact of ownership on profitability (measured by accounting ratios, ROS, ROA, and ROE), leverage (total liabilities over assets), and labour intensity. Focusing on profitability, regression results clearly point towards lower and statistically distinguishable from zero estimated coefficients for SOEs. This result suggests that, controlling for relevant firm-level variables (size and sector) along with national growth and regional and time dummies, public ownership is detrimental for firms' profitability. The results also suggest that SOEs tend to hire more labour than their private counterparts. This paper, from our perspective, has an important limitation in terms of interpretation for welfare analysis, as it does not control for price levels (and for mark-ups correlated with market concentration) when SOEs and POEs operate in a mixed oligopoly. Hence, if an SOE sells the service at a lower price than the POE, it will look as less profitable even if it covers its costs and is not loss making. It is an empirical fact that in the same market different prices are possible, particularly in network/regulated industries, for example because of incomplete information on the consumers' side. Florio (2013) for example shows that in the EU for electricity, gas, and telecommunications SOEs or partially government-invested companies over several decades tended to charge lower prices than POEs.

Wolf (2009), in a cross section of countries between 1987 and 2006, examines the differential in several output indicators, including profitability (along with production, output efficiency and revenue generation), between private and public firms in the oil industry. Empirical results clearly support the view that SOEs underperform POEs along the examined dimensions. However, using more recent and comparable data, Kowalski et al. (2013), in a paper analyzing the behaviour and role of SOEs in an international trade perspective, provide a descriptive statistical comparison of profitability of public versus private firms in the sample of Forbes Global 2000 list. Large state-owned firms are similar to their private counterparts when profitability is measured by means of ROE; they outperform private firms in terms of ROS and underperform if ROA is considered instead. Similar results were obtained by Bernier et al. (2020b), who found that

SOEs belonging to the Forbes 2000 list have higher ROS than all the Forbes 2000 firms, suggesting that they are outperforming private firms, while ROA is lower. Comparison based on ROA and cost share, computed as operational costs as share of sales revenue, is at the basis of an econometric analysis of Norwegian firms in 1999 (Christiansen and Kim 2014). The authors, while providing evidence of the increasing role of SOEs in the marketplace over the previous decade, compare the performance of private and public enterprises in five sectors (air transportation, electricity, mining, oil & gas, and telecommunication) using data for 2013 from the Forbes Global 2000 list of companies, showing that SOEs have generally exhibited higher rates of return with respect to POEs.

This reverses the message in the previous literature in the wake of Dewenter and Malatesta (2001) and the same question should be asked: are now SOEs leveraging on higher market power to earn rents? Or are they able to earn good returns and still charge lower prices than their private counterparts?

Lazzarini and Musacchio (2018) show that the performance of listed SOEs, compared by matching techniques to their relevant private counterparts, is similar, except in the case of severe recessions or similar shocks (see Box 6). Their analyzed sample, made up of 477 SOEs that are listed on the stock markets in sixty-six countries, between 1997 and 2012, exhibits similar ROA and Tobin's q with respect to privately owned firms. These findings are obtained by means of a difference-in-difference estimation and static and dynamic panel methods. This finding is robust to different definitions of ownership, including majority and minority state-ownership, and across different industries, hence it is more convincing than other studies which are more descriptive.

Goldeng et al. (2008) examine the effect of ownership on ROA and on costs relative to sales revenue, along with other relevant controls at the firm level (size, age, sector, location) and at the more aggregate level (market structure) using data for registered firms in Norway during the 1990s. Taking these metrics into consideration, state-ownership, when measured as an indicator variable, is associated, all else being equal, with inferior performance compared to private ownership. Chan et al. (2018) consider New Zealand's SOEs and a comparable sample of POEs between 1990 and 2010 in different sectors, and examine within a cross-sectional and panel setting, ROA, ROE, and Return on Revenue (ROR, computed as earnings before interest and tax divided by net revenue), along with asset and labour turnover, and labour intensity. Strong and unequivocal results are reported for ROA and ROR, consistently lower for SOEs. Kabaciński et al. (2020) consider large Polish SOEs between 2013 and 2015. Estimation of their empirical model reveals that SOEs outperform private firms when considering ROA and are indistinguishable from them when considering the EBIT (earnings before interest and taxes) margin. Szarzec and

Box 6 Comparing SOEs and POEs performance amid exogenous environmental change

Matching methods discussed in Box 5 are useful when the "selection on observables" assumption holds, that is, when the treated group and the control group differ only by a set of observable characteristics. Any bias due to unobservable factors need alternative approaches. If state ownership was a time-variant variable, this would motivate the use of panel data and fixed effect models. Unfortunately, state ownership is typically (quasi-)time invariant so that firm fixed effects would absorb (most of) the ownership effect of our interest. This is equivalent to saying that it is impossible to apply a difference-in-differences approach within this framework, since it is not possible to observe most of the treated (SOEs) before and after the treatment (change in ownership). In addition, any changes in ownership are likely to be endogenous, adding concerns of biased estimates.

However, some empirical analyses (see, e.g., Lazzarini and Musacchio 2018) have managed to extract useful information on the state-ownership effect by assessing the performance of SOEs in the context of an exogenous environmental change. In this case, it is possible to resort to a model of the following type:

$$Y_{it} = \alpha EC_{cst} + \beta SOE_i \cdot EC_{cst} + \sum_{j=1}^{J} \gamma_j Z_{ijt} \\ + \sum_{c=1}^{C} \delta_c W_{ict} + \sum_{s=1}^{S} \eta_s V_{ist} + u_i + f_t + \varepsilon_{it} \qquad (2)$$

where EC_{cst} is the variable measuring a specific event at the country-industry-year level, that is, the environmental change of interest. As the interaction term with SOE_i is time-variant, it is now possible to include firm fixed effects, u_i, to control for unobserved heterogeneity. Time fixed effects, f_t, can also be included to capture time-specific effects. All other time-variant controls can be retained in the equation. In this framework, the coefficient α represents the effect of a particular event on the performance of POEs, while the coefficient β captures the *differential effect of state-ownership* as a consequence of the event itself.

While this approach does not allow for the assessment of the state-ownership effect before the event of interest (since the non-interacted term SOE_i is absorbed by firm fixed effects), it enables the measurement of the differential effect of state ownership during the event. For instance, Lazzarini and Musacchio (2018) employ this strategy to demonstrate that severe recessions decrease the profitability of SOEs compared to

> **Box 6 (cont.)**
>
> similar POEs. This highlights how the profitability of SOEs needs to be balanced against the social and political objectives that governments seek to pursue through their ownership. Frigerio and Vandone (2020) employ a similar approach to analyze the lending activities of state-owned development banks during electoral cycles and assess whether political opportunism exists in their operations.
>
> Source: The authors, adapted from Lazzarini and Musacchio (2018).

Nowara (2017) analyze the largest firms in Central and Eastern Europe between 2007 and 2013 across different non-financial sectors and find that SOEs are substantially comparable to POEs when looking at several measures of performance. De Lange and Merlevede (2020) create a dataset of European firms across different sectors between 2002 and 2012 with detailed information on ownership and find, by looking at a series of real and financial performance indicators, that SOEs are outperformed systematically by POEs. However, they also show how the negative relationship between performance and public ownership can be mitigated in countries with good institutional quality, which is the subject of Section 3.2. Ben-Nasr (2016) indicates that in government-controlled firms, shareholders attribute diminished importance to augmenting net working capital (NWC). This is evidenced by the observation that an increase in excess-NWC is correlated with a less substantial rise in firm value, particularly for government-controlled firms with a low level of NWC investment. Using a sample of European firms Jaslowitzer et al. (2018) empirically test the relationship between state ownership and corporate investments opportunities measured by Tobin's Q and find that state-owned firms invest considerably less and in a way that is significantly less responsive to changes in investment opportunities.

The effects of state ownership can vary depending on the phases of the economic cycle. For instance, Borisova et al. (2015) observed that government ownership is typically linked to a higher cost of debt in normal economic conditions. However, during financial crises, when implicit government guarantees take precedence, state ownership becomes associated with a lower cost of debt. In a similar vein, Beuselinck et al. (2017) demonstrated that SOEs experienced a comparatively smaller decline in stock value compared to POEs in the aftermath of the Global Financial Crisis.

Bozec et al. (2006), however, shed serious doubts on the validity of comparisons between POEs and SOEs based on profitability measures due to the fact that results might depend on the objectives of the firms that are being compared. They suggest performing this type of analysis by considering productivity measures, which is the object of the following subsection. We tend to agree with them based on the theoretical arguments presented in Section 2, although some caveats are in order since productivity may also be a biased measure from a welfare analysis perspective.

3.1.2 Productivity

Economists often argue that the most relevant empirical measure of firm performance is productivity which reflects a firm's ability to use inputs in production efficiently and intensely (Comin 2010). The natural empirical indicator is total factor productivity (TFP), that is, the residual of a production function (Chambers 1988), or the portion of output not explained by the quantity of inputs used in production. In what follows, selected studies analyzing the effect of public ownership in different countries, sectors, and time periods will be surveyed, with the aim of providing an overview of contributions studying the impact of state-ownership on TFP.

There are however some caveats to be considered. Firstly, most empirical methods estimating TFP are constrained by the fact that data on input and output in physical terms are not available, hence proxies are used starting from accounting data on revenues and costs. Unfortunately, these may be affected, on the revenue side, by the issue of price distortion, which may also be relevant on the cost side: to repeat our argument, as observed prices are not shadow prices, TFP measures at market prices share the problems highlighted when discussing profitability indicators, even if their impact is somewhat mitigated if the econometrician is aware of the problem and controls for price levels. On this issue, see Box 7.

Taking advantage of the widespread wave of privatization since the 1980s, Megginson and Netter (2001) and Megginson (2005), document a productivity advantage of POEs with respect to SOEs. A possible explanation is set forward in Bai et al. (2000) who stress how often SOEs are providers of social welfare. Given the double task of reaching productive efficiency and social welfare provision, SOEs are given a low profit incentive, leading to lower performance with respect to their private counterparts. Boardman et al. (2016) studies the enduring impacts of privatization on productivity, focusing on privatizations in Canada. The key finding reveals a rising trend in the productivity of privatized state-owned enterprises relative to SOEs, although the productivity of privatized firms continues to mimic that of consistently private entities. A different conclusion is set forth by Willner (2001) who, considering ownership per se, not related to privatization, finds no significant impact of public ownership on firms' productivity. A comprehensive review of the empirical evidence on private and public enterprises' efficiency reinforces this finding, stating that 'research does not

Box 7 TFP MEASUREMENT METHODOLOGIES AND LIMITATIONS IN THE SOEs LITERATURE

TFP measures at the firm level can be derived from firm-level production functions. Addressing various econometric challenges associated with TFP estimation (for a recent overview, see Van Biesebroek, 2008, Van Beveren, 2012), three distinct methodologies can be employed. In the first estimation approach, TFP is derived from a Cobb–Douglas and *translog* production function: $y_{it} = \beta_0 + \beta_k k_{it} + \beta_l l_{it} + \beta_m z_{it} + v_i + u_{it}$. Typically, the output (y) is proxied by *operating revenues*, capital input (k) by *tangible fixed assets*, labour input (l) by *employees*, and intermediate inputs (z) by *material costs*. The lowercase letters represent natural logarithms. After estimating the production function by OLS with fixed effects, a measure of TFP is derived as the residual of the estimated production function: $TFP = \exp(\hat{\beta}_0 + \hat{v}_i + \hat{u}_{it}) = \exp(\hat{\omega}_i + \hat{u}_{it})$, where ω_i is firm-level unobserved productivity, and u_{it} denotes unexpected deviations from the mean.

An expanded variation of this methodology (Berndt and Christensen, 1973) involves adopting a *translog* production function that accommodates complementarities between labour and capital, as well as substitutability between capital and materials:

$$y_{it} = \beta_0 + \beta_k k_{it} + \beta_l l_{it} + \beta_m z_{it} + \beta_{ll} l_{it}^2 + \beta_{lk} l_{it} k_{it} + \beta_{lz} l_{it} z_{it} + \beta_{kk} k_{it}^2 + \beta_{kz} k_{it} z_{it} + \beta_{zz} z_{it}^2 + v_i + u_{it}$$

A third measurement approach is derived by employing the Levinsohn and Petrin (2003) methodology. In this context, intermediate inputs serve as a proxy for firm-level productivity shocks. This strategy is designed to address potential simultaneity issues that may arise when unobserved productivity shocks influence firms' choices of inputs. Finally, Ackerberg et al. (2015) highlight how the Olley and Pakes (1996) and Levinsohn and Petrin (2003) TFP estimation techniques may suffer from functional dependence problems that lead to a non-identification of the labour coefficient in the first stages and propose an alternative approach.

Estimation of TFP from revenue-based data, rather than quantity data, may also suffer from input-price bias, that is, the bias that arises from unobserved (by the analyst) input prices by firms. Another potential bias can arise in the case of multi-product firms from the unobserved allocation of inputs across different product. De Loecker et al. (2016), propose a method to overcome these biases. Regardless of the methodology

> **Box 7 (cont.)**
>
> employed, the TFP measures discussed are susceptible to fluctuations in input and output prices as they are based on balance-sheet data (revenue and cost values). This characteristic diminishes their appropriateness for discerning and contrasting the inherent efficiency or productivity distinctions between SOEs and POEs, since the pricing mechanisms, cost structures, subsidies, and regulatory constraints encountered by SOEs typically differ from those faced by their private counterparts (see Section 2). Consequently, the relevant balance-sheet data are defined through possibly distorted prices. It is essential to acknowledge that econometric analysis comparing the productivity of SOEs and POEs encounter this limitation. To overcome this challenge, alternative measures or adjustments to TFP calculations should be considered to effectively account for contextual variations, but the empirical literature in this direction is still scant.
>
> Source: The authors, adapted from Borghi et al. (2016) and Castelnovo et al. (2019).

support the conclusion that privately owned firms are more efficient than otherwise-comparable state-owned firms' (Mühlenkamp 2015, p. 553).

A first, tentative answer to the initial question of whether ownership matters for firm-level performance, measured now by TFP, is that there is no compelling evidence in favour of the widely held view that POEs are more productive than SOEs, but there is no evidence to the contrary either. Does this line of reasoning hold also when considering firms belonging to one sector at a time?

Moving away from cross-sectoral studies, several authors have analyzed POEs and SOEs within specific sectors, mainly within network industries, where state-ownership is still widespread. Kwoka (2005) starts from the premise that previous studies comparing the effect of ownership on firms' performance and profitability had provided mixed evidence. By focusing on the electricity utilities sector in the United States, the author demonstrates how sectoral issues matter. SOEs in the distribution segment of the industry have an advantage over POEs due to the quality issues related to the product, while POEs exhibit higher cost-efficiency in the generation segment. Focusing on the electricity retail sector in Germany, Stiel et al. (2018) do not find any evidence that SOEs or POEs are different in terms of firm-level productivity. Moving on to the transport sector, Backx et al. (2002) introduces the role of the percentage of state-ownership in shaping the effect on productivity. By analyzing the airline industry, the authors find, using panel data between 1993 and 1997 for a sample of international medium-large passenger airlines, that public ownership is detrimental to firm-level efficiency, and that this effect increases as the percentage of public ownership increases. Dalen and Gómez-Lobo (2003) consider the Norwegian bus industry with a sample of 142 companies over the 1987–1997 period. Singling out the results related to public versus private ownership, the authors document that SOEs are more cost-efficient with respect to their private counterparts. A set of potential explanations are put forward, including economies of scale and scope (evidence of the latter provided, among others, by Growitsch and Wetzel (2009) for the railway sector), specifically related to the characteristics of the sector under consideration, and the fact that SOEs could be intrinsically more efficient than POEs. Roy and Yvrande-Billon (2007), using data from 1995 to 2002 for firms in the French urban transport networks, show that public administrations and semi-public enterprises exhibit lower levels of technical efficiency than fully private ones, with mixed ownership entities being the most inefficient. Boitani et al. (2013), using data on urban local public transport in European cities between 1997 and 2006 find that majority and minority SOEs exhibit lower productivity than POEs, while also suggesting the importance of competitive tendering (see Section 3.2). Díaz and Charles (2016) examine the provision of local public transport in France and find that private operators are more efficient than public ones, but less efficient than mixed ownership operators. Explicit consideration of the type of contractual agreements governing the type of contract makes ownership less relevant in explaining differences in efficiencies, as these are almost fully accounted for by contractual issues. Eller et al. (2011) compare the productivity of national and private international oil companies (NOCs and IOCs, respectively), finding that NOCs are less efficient than IOCs, this result primarily driven by internal institutional features, mainly related to differing objectives, within the firms.

Abbot and Cohen (2009) perform a literature review on the determinants of productivity in the water sector, focusing on studies up to the end of the 2000s. Focusing on their analysis of the impact of ownership, what emerges from existing literature is a blurred picture, with some studies documenting that SOEs are more efficient than POEs in this sector, while others find the opposite result. These mixed findings might be related, according to the authors, to two possible explanations. First, ownership matters less for firm-level productivity in the water sector than corporatization, which could be the main driver of improvements. Second, the water supply sector is characterized by monopoly features that allow productivity improvements only through regulation. Le Lannier and Porcher (2014) consider a cross section of the largest water services in France in 2009 and analyze the determinants of TFP for 117 firms. With respect to ownership, results point to a productivity advantage of SOEs, which are at least in part explained by the different approach to water conservation and differences in the water budget debt between private and public firms. Suárez-Varela et al. (2017) use data for 2013 of firms providing Spanish municipalities with water services. Ownership is not neutral with respect to productivity and the analysis provides interesting results. Private providers tend to be technically more efficient that public ones when the management of the labour input is considered, a result that can be explained with the well-known labour hoarding hypothesis in state-owned firms in general, and when considering price efficiency. On the contrary, public ownership is associated with higher cost-efficiency. A different result is suggested by Walter et al. (2009) in their interesting meta-analysis of the benchmarking of the water distribution sector. Their analyses suggest that there is no evidence of a clear impact of public or private ownership, while the main driver of efficiency is the institutional setting.

A tentative conclusion from sectoral studies is that, in general, SOEs in network industries seem to be performing similarly or even outperforming POEs. One explanation for this result lies in the specificities of these sectors, which might favour vertical integration and where the role of competition is overall limited, pointing to mixed oligopoly. In turn, the theoretical models on mixed oligopoly mentioned in Section 2.7 overall do not suggest that productivity should systematically differ between public and private market players. The assumption in those models that SOE have a social welfare objective has implications for setting prices (and quality) but not for cost minimization by managerial teams. Hence the empirical results do not contradict most mixed oligopoly models.

However, taken as a whole, the surveyed literature provides varying evidence to the ownership-productivity nexus, which might go beyond the varying sectoral, geographic, and temporal coverage of the different studies. A growing body of research has been focusing on the relevance of a set of context conditions, external to the firm, the inclusion of which in the empirical analyses might in fact help disentangle the conflicting evidence surveyed here (see also Section 3.2).

3.1.3 R&D and Innovation Policy

SOEs can also be interpreted with respect to their role in pursuing public goals, thus becoming instruments of public policy, or more specifically of innovation policy (Tõnurist and Karo 2016, Benassi and Landoni 2019, Meissner et al. 2019,), foreign policy (Miroudot and Ragoussis 2011, Musacchio et al. 2015), environmental policy (Christiansen 2013), along with the general contribution to social welfare through employment (Bridgman and Greenaway-McGrevy 2022), and the provision of services of general interest at fair prices (Florio 2013), to name a few.

We discuss each of these issues, starting with innovation, that was included in the discussion in the previous section, see Section 2.9. While the focus there was on the concept of research infrastructures, SOEs may be willing to invest in R&D more than POEs as knowledge creation may be seen as part of their public mission.

When analyzing the role that SOEs can play in terms of promoting innovation, Sterlacchini (2012), taking into account the specificities of network industries, examines the electricity sector to understand the relationship between public ownership and innovation. Focusing on the world's major companies, in terms of electricity generation, between 2000 and 2008, empirical results suggest that SOEs tend to have a higher R&D over sales ratio when compared to relevant POEs in the same sector, and in a context of decreasing R&D figures, have experienced a less pronounced decline in this measure. Within the same sector, Tõnurist (2015) proposes a case-study on a major Estonian electricity company, suggesting that, in order for SOEs to be effective as instruments of innovation policy, short-term goals are detrimental. Tõnurist and Karo (2016) suggest that these shortfalls can be overcome by means of appropriate policy coordination within innovation systems and by specific actions financing innovation.

A standard indicator of innovation is filing patents. Indeed, patents are not only publicly available documents collected on a regular basis, but they are also characterized by the presence of very long historical time series and typically display a high correlation with other measures of innovative performance at the firm level, such as R&D spending and new product announcements. Jamasb and Pollitt (2011) analyze the patenting activity of UK electricity firms and show that after the liberalization reforms there has been a reduction of R&D investments, with a consequent a drop in the number of patents filed by firms, except for patents in non-nuclear and renewable technologies, which increased in the post-liberalization period thanks to strategic subsidies. In more recent years, the authors highlight a significant recovery in R&D expenditure due to the implementation of effective innovation policies and an improved institutional framework (Jamasb and Pollitt 2015). Bortolotti et al. (2019) consider both R&D spending and patents for European listed firms between 2000 and 2009, finding mixed results. SOEs invest more in R&D than private firms if political variables are not controlled for, due to easier access to credit, while they produce fewer patents per dollar invested, but with more citations than their private counterparts.

Clò et al. (2020) examine the telecommunications industry (TLC) and investigate the potential role of enterprises under public control as active players in technological creation. Their key outcome variable is the total number of patent applications filed every year by each company; results show that in state-invested enterprises (i.e., enterprises under public control) public ownership is positively correlated to patenting activity, and this relationship is stronger for SOEs in countries with high-quality government and institutions, where state-owned companies benefit from improved governance mechanisms (i.e., being subjected to less political interference in the appointment of managers and of transparency of the public mission that is assigned to them) and depart from the short-term profit goal of private enterprises.

Similar results are in Lazzarini et al. (2021). The authors focus on a worldwide and cross-industry sample of large SOEs and POEs with the aim of analyzing their capacity to create new inventions. Results show that SOEs – especially those operating in high innovation industries – invent more intensively (i.e., file more patents) than private firms, and produce more pioneering inventions (i.e., file more patents that do not cite any other previously patented work). They also found that institutional and industry features influence SOEs innovative performance: a strong institutional environment in the home country (i.e., improved checks and balances against governmental intervention), increases the intensity, originality, and impact of SOEs' inventions.

Patent activity of SOEs is analyzed also in Castelnovo (2022), who takes a cross-industry perspective and provides empirical evidence on the innovation performance of a sample of European state-owned companies. Results reveal that in high R&D intensive industries the innovative performance of SOEs is superior to those of POEs, entailing that the innovation policies could take advantage from SOEs as a vehicle of technological development and contributor to long-term economic growth.

3.1.4 Internationalization and Foreign Policy

SOEs are increasingly moving beyond their national boundaries by engaging in international trade of both goods and services, and by being active players in the international mergers and acquisitions (M&A) market. Some authors have indeed highlighted how SOEs are becoming, for some governments, instruments of foreign policy, thus identifying an additional objective that SOE managers must achieve. A preliminary issue is whether ownership matters when examining deals in the M&A market (both domestic and international), as documented by D'Souza and Nash (2017). Clò et al. (2017b) present evidence supporting that ownership matters in the international M&A market, with SOEs (defined as state majority owned firms) acquiring lower performing targets with respect to POEs. Minority owned state enterprises instead behave as POEs, hinting towards the possibility that SOEs internalize political objectives. Along similar lines, Del Bo et al. (2017) show that SOEs deviate from the benchmark of deals involving private firms on both sides of the M&A transaction.

Benito et al. (2016) examine whether the gains from internationalization change with state or private ownership of publicly listed Norwegian companies between 2000 and 2010. Theoretically, SOEs are shown to have more to gain from internationalization than POEs but their ability to reap these potential benefits, in terms of higher ROS, ROA and Tobin's q, are hindered by their non-economic objectives and corporate deficiencies. However, empirical results do not provide compelling evidence of greater benefits for SOEs but show that initially domestically oriented SOEs gain more from internationalization and learn to adapt to markets. Clifton et al. (2016) explore the issue of whether entering foreign markets causes a dilution of SOEs' public values. By adopting the point of view of the international shareholder, the authors examine the behaviour and public values of the world's major public utility multinationals. Their analysis sheds doubt on the possibility that public values can be transferred to foreign markets when a utilities SOE goes abroad, as profit maximization trumps other objectives.

A strand of literature has been analyzing the behaviour of SOEs when entering the foreign M&A market and the determinants of their strategies and results (Del Bo et al. 2017). Karolyi and Liao (2017) examine 4759 cross-border acquisitions to understand the difference that can be attributed to state ownership. A key result is that privately and publicly owned acquirers behave differently in terms of targets, strategies, and results of deals. The empirical analysis suggests that, on average, SOEs acting as acquirers are more likely than their private counterparts to come from autocratic countries, tend to aim at deals that involve total acquisition of the target, have higher announcement returns, and no higher likelihood of deal failure or withdrawal. Jory and Ngo (2014), examining a sample of US firms acquiring targets abroad between 1987 and 2009 show that bidders of SOEs underperform bidders of POEs in terms of both stock price and operating performance. They further qualify their results by considering the level of institutional quality in the target's country, finding that bidders tend to acquire SOEs in countries with low institutional quality. This in turn affects the acquirers' performance. Kalasin (2020) examines the mechanism through which public ownership influences the internationalization strategies of firms, suggesting an S shaped relationship, with low and high degrees of public ownership exhibiting a lower degree of internationalization with respect to mixed ownership firms. Del Bo et al. (2017) also consider whether bidders are SOEs or POEs, and find that publicly owned firms tend to target higher quality firms to acquire. Holland (2019) explicitly examines the role of governments as investors, showing that the average investor reaction is positive and shareholder wealth increases, although different types of government investors (political, financial, and industrial) elicit different market reactions. Grøgaard et al. (2019)

show that SOEs and POEs tend to behave differently when acting as acquirers, with SOEs acquiring stand-alone assets or a smaller proportion of shares, but also highlight how these differences tend to be mitigated when home countries are characterized by high institutional quality and market orientation, a result that hints to the discussion in Section 3.2.

3.1.5 Environmental Policies and Sustainability

SOEs could also be vehicles of environmental policies and have sustainability objectives (see Section 2.9). One of the first empirical evaluations of this potential role is performed by Meyer and Pac (2013) considering the electricity sector in Europe. By comparing the environmental performance, in terms of plant level emissions of sulphur dioxide of state-owned and privatized energy utility plants in Eastern Europe, the authors show that SOEs tend to have higher levels of emissions than private firms.

More recent studies, however, have found evidence in favour of a role for SOEs in increasing environmental sustainability. Earnhart and Lizal (2006), for example provide support for the hypothesis that, in the Czech Republic, state ownership is beneficial, in terms of environmental performance with respect to other ownership types. Calza et al. (2016), using cross-sectional data on European firms included into the Carbon Disclosure Project questionnaire 2012, provide evidence that firms with a higher percentage of state ownership present superior green proactivity. Clò et al. (2017a), analyzes how ownership affects the environmental performance by looking at a cross-country panel dataset of European's power companies over the period 1990–2012. The authors measures the environmental performance with both greenhouse gas emissions and carbon intensity and find that public ownership is associated with lower emissions than private ownership. Their results are consistent with the theoretical model where it is assumed that in developed countries, when there is social demand for environmental protection, enterprises controlled by the government internalize an environmental goal in their objective function.

These results are in line with the rising relevance in the European political agenda of the issue of climate change mitigation, which is particularly relevant for SOEs and their public purpose (Marois 2022), as well as with some recent recommendations of the European Commission related to corporate decision-makers' duties and sustainability[8] according to which embedding environmental, social and

---

[8] European Commission, "Action Plan: Financing Sustainable Growth COM (2018) 97 final", March 2018; EU, "Study on directors' duties and sustainable corporate governance", July 2020 (report prepared for the European Commission DG Justice and Consumers); EU consultation on "Sustainable Corporate Governance"; Revision of Directive 2014/95/EU "Non-Financial Reporting Directive".

governance-related risks (ESG) issues in the business strategy not only helps reducing sustainability related risks and negative impacts, but also move the business beyond short-term focus and create value in the long term. In fact, the literature connects short-termism to unsatisfactory response to environmental issues both at individual and organizational level (Slawinski et al. 2017, Sjafjell 2018), while climate change mitigation requires significant upfront investments by the companies.

3.1.6 Prices and Quality

The relationship between ownership network industries and social welfare can also be examined by considering whether private and public enterprises differ in terms of the price and quality at which they provide goods and services. Starting from price issues, Brau et al. (2010) analyze the impact of reforms in the natural gas industry on consumer prices across the EU-15 area using data between 1991 and 2007. Their results on the relationship between ownership and prices suggest that, in the European gas industry, SOEs charge lower prices than their private counterparts. Growitsch and Stronzik (2014), using data on a slightly larger sample of European countries, confirm that privatization leads to higher prices. Considering the electricity sector, Fiorio and Florio (2013) study the impact of corporate ownership on residential electricity prices, separating it from the liberalization effect and report that public ownership is associated with lower residential electricity prices in Western Europe between 1991 and 2007. Similarly, del-Río, Fernández-Sainz and Alegria (2019), who focus instead on industrial electricity prices in Europe between 2003 and 2013, find that SOEs offer electricity to industrial customers at lower prices than private ones. Bacchiocchi et al. (2011) examine another network industry, namely TLC, and find that ownership is irrelevant with respect to price levels for international and national call prices, while it is higher when considering local calls. Recently, Calzada and Díaz-Serrano (2023) examine the interrelations between regulatory reforms in the TLC industry and the creation of the European single market and highlight how public or private ownership is not statistically different from zero price differences. Taken together, these contributions suggest that, at least when considering the liberalization and reform package that was introduced in Europe starting in the 1990s, prices in network industries are lower, or at least not higher, in the presence of public, rather than private, ownership.

Considering another important aspect in terms of social welfare, quality of services and customer satisfaction is, on average, higher when providers are SOEs, as documented by Bacchiocchi et al. (2011) for TLC and Fiorio and Florio (2011) for electricity.

The picture that emerges from this literature confirms the idea that SOEs might be invested of broader goals and objectives than simple profit maximization or technical efficiency, and this aspect should be taken into account when performing comparisons between private and state-owned firms based on simple performance indicators, as highlighted in Section 2.3.

3.2 The Role of Contextual Factors: Institutions, Regulation, and Politics

The most recent empirical literature has focused on the role of external factors in shaping the effect on firms' activities and behaviour of ownership, including market structure and related reforms, regulation, political factors and, increasingly, the institutional setting in which firms operate (see Box 8). According to North (1991), "institutions are the humanly devised constraints that structure political, economic, and social interaction". Indeed, all the human interactions take place within the choice set defined by the current institutional framework.

Focusing on market structure, Asaftei et al. (2008) consider Romanian firms between 1995 and 2003 and verify whether state ownership is detrimental, or not, to productivity. Their results hint towards the importance of the environment in which firms operate since private firms indeed appear to exhibit higher efficiency levels than state-owned ones in highly competitive sectors but not in sectors with lower degrees of competition. Examining the role of regulatory reforms, Scheffler et al. (2013) examine the role of market reforms and regulation along with ownership on German bus transport companies. Their empirical results suggest that firms operating in regions where competitive tendering takes place are more efficient than those in regions that have not implemented these reforms, while ownership per se does not matter.

Another relevant strand of literature has focused on the impact of institutional quality and specific dimensions, such as for example corruption, on firm-level performance and how these factors influence the role of state versus private ownership. Driffield et al. (2013) introduce ownership as a factor influencing the impact of external institutional quality on firms' performance and find that institutional reforms leading to increased country level competition influences mainly state-owned firms. Belloc (2014) suggests that, contrary to the conventional wisdom, SOEs' inefficiency is not due to state ownership per se but is likely related to other conditions, such as institutions, culture, legislation, and the degree of political competition. Dal Bo and Rossi (2007) present a theoretical model examining the link between corruption and firm-level efficiency between 1994 and 2001 and test its predictions with data on the efficiency of electricity distribution firms in Latin America. Their main result is that indeed national-level corruption is associated with firm-level inefficiency; specifically, firms in

Box 8 Institutional quality as a mediating factor

Economic theory posits that effective institutions can play a crucial role in alleviating distortions linked to opportunistic behaviour and rent seeking, thereby tempering adverse government interference in SOEs. Accordingly, scholarly focus within the empirical literature has progressively pivoted towards investigating the impact of the institutional framework on the operations and outcomes of SOEs. A prevalent research hypothesis suggests that SOEs located in countries characterized by robust institutional quality are likely to exhibit improved managerial efficiency, leading to a diminished probability of markedly inferior firm performance, irrespective of the performance metric employed.

To test this proposition, we augment the baseline model (1) presented in Box 4 with two additional variables: the level of institutional quality (IQ_c) and the interaction term between state ownership and institutional quality ($SOE_i \cdot IQ_c$). The extended model is expressed as follows:

$$Y_i = \alpha + \beta SOE_i + \theta IQ_c + \varphi SOE_i \cdot IQ_c + \sum\nolimits_{j=1}^{J} \gamma_j Z_{ij} + \sum\nolimits_{c=1}^{C} \delta_c W_{ic} + \sum\nolimits_{s=1}^{S} \eta_s V_{is} + \varepsilon_i \qquad (3)$$

Here, θ captures the influence of institutional quality on firm performance, irrespective of ownership structure, while φ measures the mediating effect of institutional quality on the relationship between state ownership and firm performance. This analytical approach enables the estimation of the marginal effect of state ownership, represented as:

$$\frac{\partial Y_i}{\partial SOE_i} = \beta + \varphi \cdot IQ_c \qquad (4)$$

If $\beta < 0$ and $\varphi > 0$, it would signify that a positive effect of state ownership is contingent upon institutional quality (IQ_c) exceeding a certain threshold, specifically, $IQ_c > -\frac{\beta}{\varphi}$.

The same rationale prompts the introduction of a triple interaction term in the model [2] presented in Box 5:

$$Y_{it} = \alpha EC_{cst} + \theta IQ_{ct} + \lambda EC_{cst} \cdot IQ_{ct} + \beta SOE_i \cdot EC_{cst} + \varphi SOE_i \cdot IQ_{ct} + \rho SOE_i \cdot EC_{cst} \cdot IQ_{ct} + \sum\nolimits_{j=1}^{J} \gamma_j Z_{ijt} + \sum\nolimits_{c=1}^{C} \delta_c W_{ict} + \sum\nolimits_{s=1}^{S} \eta_s V_{ist} + u_i + f_t + \varepsilon_{it} \qquad (5)$$

> **Box 8 (cont.)**
>
> In this context, the coefficient ρ provides insights into whether heightened institutional development serves to mitigate potential performance differentials between SOEs and POEs, contingent upon specific environmental changes (events).
>
> Commonly employed metrics for assessing institutional quality in empirical economic literature include, among many others: the Quality of Government index sourced from the International Country Risk Guide; regulatory quality (Kaufmann et al. 2010); government effectiveness (Kaufmann et al. 2010); political constraints (Henisz 2000, 2002).
>
> Source: The authors, adapted from Borghi et al. (2016) and Lazzarini and Musacchio (2018).

more corrupt countries tend to use more labour to produce a certain level of output. Additionally, the authors report that SOEs are, on average, less efficient than POEs, but do not test the mediating effect corruption could have on this relationship. This latter aspect is specifically tackled in Borghi et al. (2016) and Castelnovo et al. (2019), who examine the interplay between internal (ownership) and external factors (institutional quality) on firm-level TFP, respectively in the European electricity (2002–2009 period) and telecommunications sector (2007–2015 period). By focusing on the interaction between public ownership and different measures of institutional quality, the theoretical and empirical results suggest that SOEs in good institutional contexts may outperform POEs in terms of TFP. Underlying this empirical finding is the fact that a low-quality institutional environment is especially detrimental for SOEs. Recognizing the importance of different mandates and objectives for SOEs, other than efficiency, Estrin et al. (2016) consider the influence of external institutions at the national level on public enterprises' internationalization strategies. Their empirical analysis, based on a sample of 306 matched POEs and SOEs from forty countries from the Worldscope database in 2010, suggests that ownership does not affect internationalization strategies. In fact, when institutional quality is similar, the behaviour of POEs and SOEs converges. National institutions, thought of as mechanisms shaping the ability of various shareholders of influencing SOEs internationalization decisions, exert an important effect on firm behaviour. Finally, Beuselinck et al. (2017) show that in the aftermath of the global financial crisis, SOEs underwent a comparatively modest decline in stock value contrasted with POEs but only in countries with sufficiently high institutional quality.

Political factors, including political connections that SOE managers might enjoy, are the subject matter of another set of articles. In an interesting meta-analysis on the interplay of ownership and political connection on firms' strategies and performance, Tihanyi et al. (2019) examine 210 studies from 139 countries. Focusing primarily on the management literature, the authors find that political connections have no consequences for firm-level performance, while public ownership has a small negative effect. The most interesting result, however, is the fact that both state ownership and political connections influence firms' strategies in areas such as financial leverage, the level of R&D intensity, and internationalization. Further, the authors suggest that these strategies have a mediating effect on the ownership–performance relation, thus suggesting relevant indirect channels through which being public or private and the interplay with political factors influence firm-level performance. Inoue (2020) develops a conceptual model on the link between performance of SOEs and political incentives of managers. Using data from the water sector in Brazil with data on 2282 private and public enterprises between 2004 and 2014, the author shows how employment is higher and financial performance (measured by ROS) is worse, respectively, in election years, suggesting that SOE performance is contingent on political cycles and thus varies over time. Adua and Clark (2021) consider the impact of political partisanship on state-level utilities' investment in energy efficiency in the United States in 2015. Examining the price setting behaviour of local district heating utilities in Sweden between 1998 and 2007, Biggar and Söderberg (2020) show that political ideology at the municipal level has an impact on pricing, with left-wing local governments smoothing prices over time, while there is no clear systematic difference between private and public firms. Coulomb and Sangnier (2014) analyze the effect of being linked to France's two presidential candidates in 2007 (in the sense of being part of their respective personal networks or firms being expected to benefit from their election) on firms' abnormal returns. While the authors find strong evidence of an impact of political ties on returns, their results also show how political majorities does not operate primarily via state ownership of firms, since there is no detectable difference between private and state-owned firms. Qingyuan et al. (2020) investigates the investment behaviours of European SOEs around national elections between 2001 and 2015. The authors find that SOEs increase their corporate investment during national election years and the effect is also stronger in countries with low institutional quality, more centralized political systems, and state-controlled banking systems.

Aguilera et al. (2021) add another dimension and consider the interplay of political ideology and institutional quality on the nexus between ownership and productivity. By means of a meta-analysis of an international sample of 193 studies on the ownership–performance relation, over the 1961–2003 period from 131 countries, the authors reach interesting results. First, the survey of the literature documents a small negative effect of state ownership on financial performance, with high heterogeneity both in terms of geography and size of the estimated effect. Second, both the government's political ideology and institutions at the country level have a relevant effect on the ability of state owners of achieving both business and social goals. In countries with right-wing governments, SOEs are characterized by higher performance than in left-wing governed countries. Additionally, SOEs tend to perform better if the institutional quality is high, leading to low levels of political constraints for SOEs' managers.

Soft-budget constraints, which have been frequently cited as characterizing the governance of SOEs (Kornai 1992), can also be seen as external institutional factors which might influence the performance of SOEs, as highlighted in Section 2.5. By examining initially post-Soviet countries in Eastern Europe, soft-budget constraints can be thought of in terms of, for example, state subsidies, soft taxation, non-performing loans, the accumulation of trade arrears between firms, and the build-up of wage arrears (Kornai 2001). The presence of various degrees of soft-budget constraints would thus help explain the estimated lower performance of SOEs with respect to their private counterparts, which was incorrectly attributed to ownership. Bertero and Rondi (2002) empirically address this issue by considering a regime change in Italian law, which brought a hardening of the budget constraint for SOEs in 1987. The empirical analysis on a panel of 150 Italian SOEs between 1977 to 1993 shows that under the soft-budget regime, investment is positively and significantly related to cash flow and that the regime shift leads to the disappearance of this relationship, suggesting that indeed a soft-budget constraint regime could lead to over investment and, consequently, to lower performance levels.

Taken together, these contributions on external factors highlight the importance these exert on firm-level productivity and show how institutional, political, and regulatory aspects influence the ownership–productivity nexus. What emerges is that some of the differences in performance, productivity, and other measures of firm-level activity that have been reported in previous studies between private and public enterprises might, at least in part, be due to the impact of external contextual conditions, most notably related to institutional quality and political factors. When taking these aspects into account, the effect of ownership per se is weaker and, if present, is better understood in relation to the external institutional factors. By implication, institutions are probably the key omitted variable in most empirical analyses reported in Section 3.1.

3.3 Methodological Issues in the Empirical Analysis of SOE Performance

As shown in Table 1, earlier empirical literature on the economic performance of SOEs has predominantly relied upon a cross-sectional comparison of SOEs and POEs. Conventional ordinary least squares (OLS) approaches have been employed to estimate the regression models, typically incorporating additional regressors to account for potential confounding factors at both the firm and country levels. A notable limitation of these analyses arises from the frequent absence of comparable POEs within the same industry, country, and year for SOEs. In fact, Lazzarini and Musacchio (2018) highlight that 'only 15.6% of majority SOEs have private firms in the same country and sector'. Consequently, to address this issue, they resort to matching techniques to enhance the comparability of SOEs and POEs within their dataset, a methodological approach that could be the basis for future research on the subject.

Further analysis examine the influence of state ownership on performance by leveraging the experiences of SOEs that undergo privatization. However, in these instances, identifying the role of the state before and after privatizations poses a challenge. As highlighted by Dewenter and Malatesta (2001), alterations in firms' performance post privatization may partly stem from changes induced by governments prior to privatization. This is due to the fact that governments often initiate restructuring efforts in firms before placing them on the private market.

Panel analyses and fixed effects models have been introduced to control for unobserved heterogeneity and the resulting issues of endogeneity, wherein some time-invariant component is possibly correlated with both the dependent variable (firm performance) and the explanatory variable (likelihood of being state-owned or selected for privatization over time). A limitation of these analyses is once again the reliance on ownership changes over time (e.g., privatizations), bringing forth selection bias challenges, as mentioned earlier. Ideally, a two-stage Heckman model could be employed to address selection bias by identifying, in the first stage, the probability of a firm transitioning from SOE to POE. Nevertheless, as observed by Goldeng et al. (2008), this approach is not always feasible, depending on the coverage of available samples. Furthermore, as noted by Wolf (2009), another limitation of fixed effects regressions in this context is their ability to quantify the impact of state ownership based only on firms that have changed ownership over time. Additionally, fixed effect models do not resolve potential endogeneity due to omitted time-variant variables. In such cases, an instrumental variable (IV) approach is necessary, as seen in Meyer and Pac (2013), who employ a country political variable as an instrument, considering that the ideology of governing parties is expected to influence the likelihood of privatizations taking place.

Some analyses, such as Benito et al. (2016), also resort to *internal* instruments using lagged variables (i.e., generalized method of moments or GMM) when suitable *external* instruments are not available (see also Roodman 2009). Through a meta-analytic regression analysis, Aguilera et al. (2021) demonstrated that empirical studies controlling for endogeneity tend to reveal a positive relationship between state ownership and performance, underscoring the potential impact of reverse causality and selection effects on results of opposing signs.

Another potential limitation of the several empirical analyses is their focus on individual countries or markets. While, on the one hand, this focus is justified by the need to conduct the analysis within a sufficiently homogeneous context for comparing the performance of public and private enterprises, on the other hand, it complicates the generalization and external validity of empirical evidence.

Although more recent articles have attempted to introduce progressive methodological improvements to address the aforementioned limitations and enhance their evidence through robustness tests, some constraints are inherent to the subject matter and, consequently, to the type of available data. These limitations have contributed to fostering further developments in the empirical literature concerning SOEs, developments that we believe may yield additional insights in the near future.

Firstly, owing to the recent evolution of SOEs, an increasing number of analyses have begun to focus on continuous measures of state ownership rather than dichotomous variables. This shift has allowed for greater emphasis on the reality of hybrid organizations and public–private partnerships (see Section 3.4). From a methodological perspective, this type of analysis opens up avenues for employing various econometric tools to account for the possibility of nonlinear effects of state ownership on firm performance. For instance, regression models can incorporate quadratic terms (to capture non-monotonic effects) or interaction terms (to capture moderation effects). Alternatively, researchers can employ threshold analyses to explore the presence of critical points or breakpoints in the relationship between state ownership and firm performance.

Secondly, rather than fixating on the comparison between SOEs and POEs, the research question is evolving, particularly considering that SOEs constitute an integral part of our economic systems. Consequently, the focus is increasingly shifting towards asking, 'What are the conditions that promote the effectiveness and efficiency of SOEs?' As detailed in Section 3.5, this shift prompts attention towards comparing SOEs with different corporate governance characteristics rather than emphasizing the distinctions between SOEs and POEs. It is evident that corporate governance stands out as one of the prime candidates among the potential channels through which variations in the institutional quality at the country level affect the performance of SOEs. Methodologically, this type of analysis broadens the spectrum of identification strategies because a single enterprise, while remaining state-owned since its establishment, may still undergo significant changes in terms of corporate governance.

Finally, there is a noticeable growth in the empirical literature that, instead of dwelling on the performance of individual firms, emphasizes the characteristics of firms targeted by SOEs through M&A deals (see, for example: Clò et al. 2017b, Karolyi and Liao 2017) or the foreign direct investments made by SOEs (Grøgaard et al. 2019). Other research focuses on the spillover effects that SOEs may have on the aggregate economy. The final part (Section 3.6) provides a brief overview of some recent developments regarding the aggregate effects of state ownership on the surrounding socio-economic environment. Once again, the new focus of these analyses provides interesting methodological insights, as identification strategies can concentrate on observed differences at the aggregate level before and after the entry of SOEs into the target market or as a consequence of the intensification (or relaxation) of their activities. This type of analysis is well-suited for difference-in-differences methodologies, which in recent years have seen significant contributions and advancements. For instance, it is our opinion that difference-in-differences analyses with heterogeneous treatment (de Chaisemartin and D'Haultfoeuille 2020, 2023) can have important developments in this context since they provide robust estimators when the treatment effect is not constant between groups or over time. The review of this section indeed highlights how state-ownership can have profoundly differentiated effects depending on the reference cohort.

3.4 The Performance Effect of State Ownership: A Summary

From a bird's eye overview of Table 1, when surveying a selection of papers comparing private and public enterprises on the basis of financial and accounting measures of performance and profitability, and then total factor productivity, no crystal-clear conclusion stands out. At closer inspection, however, the following key points emerge.

A first element is related to the choice of the dependent variable, with earlier works focusing more on performance, both in terms of profitability and productivity, while an increase in the use of 'other' variables has emerged over time. The impact of ownership is increasingly examined by considering environmental outcomes, the behaviour of firms on the M&A market, and on innovation, to mention the most frequent choices.

A second consideration is that, on average, papers that consider profitability indicators report more frequently a statistically distinguishable from zero negative estimated coefficient related to state ownership, while papers focusing on 'other' variables as described above tend to report on average a positive coefficient. This latter result might suggest which objectives and areas could be targets of further research and eventually policy intervention.

In general, however, the variety of results could be explained by the different estimation methodologies employed (see Section 3.3) and by the selection of the sample in terms of sectoral or geographic composition. In fact, conclusions vary greatly by sector, suggesting that sector-specific characteristics might have a relevant effect on the relationship between ownership and firm-level performance. What should be noted is that, over time, the management and environment in which SOEs operate has changed, with the introduction of improved management practices in SOEs, in the adoption of stringent budget constraints in the public sector in general, in the effect of aggregate reforms (e.g., liberalization, corporatizations, regulation) that might benefit SOEs comparatively more than private-owned enterprises, and these reforms have been adopted at different paces and degrees in different countries. Finally, conventional wisdom viewing private firms as naturally more profitable and more productive than publicly owned entities is challenged, and in some instances reversed, when aggregate contextual conditions are considered, most notably concerning institutional quality and aggregate political factors.

Ownership matters for performance and aggregate economic activity, but is it simply the distinction between private and state ownership that we should focus on? The answer is probably negative, as hinted above, when a distinction between the behaviour of majority and minority state ownership was made and by considering that, over time (see Table 1), research has moved from a dichotomous distinction between fully private or full public enterprises to considering the continuum between the two. Several scholars (Koppell 2003, Oum et al. 2006, Christensen and Lægreid 2011, Doherty et al. 2014), in fact, have pointed towards the importance of the hybrid nature of several SOEs for understanding their behaviour, performance, and definition of their mission (Sorrentino 2020). Ownership is increasingly seen not as a dichotomous state, but as a continuum, calling for the analysis of hybrid organizations. Bruton et al. (2015) analyze four sectors across twenty-three states and provide a case-study analysis of thirty-six firms, suggesting that the emergence of hybrid organizations suggests caution when classifying firms as private or state-owned and basing performance comparisons on this dichotomy. Chen et al. (2018) consider how the hybrid nature of many SOEs affects their behaviour on international markets, by adopting a principal-principal perspective. The authors argue that the private–public agency problem present in many state-owned (at different levels) enterprises, is different from the same problem when all involved parties are private, and document the emergence of conflicts between large government and private block holders. These conflicts, in turn, affect managerial decisions, especially when these organizations enter the foreign M&A market. The definition itself of a hybrid organization is difficult to define, as this umbrella term is used for a variety of configurations, including truly mixed enterprises, public–private partnerships, social entrepreneurship organizations, government-sponsored enterprises, and several other hybrid configurations (Vining and Weimer 2016). Vining and Weimer (2017) show how the institutional arrangements for managing these hybrid organizations vary greatly across countries, sectors, and levels of government, suggesting that these enterprises are intrinsically complex in nature. Their research suggests that these types of organizations are not new, as Adam Smith had analyzed the East India Company and highlighted the issues related to its hybrid ownership nature. Vining et al. (2014) analyze hybrids at the local government level, focusing on enterprises providing local public goods, and stress how they should be driven by the goal of maximizing local social welfare.

3.5 Corporate Governance

A relatively recent body of literature focuses on corporate governance and analyzes the role of the board of directors in managing SOEs and addressing their weaknesses. Indeed, while board composition has been a highly studied topic as far as private firms are concerned, it has received little attention in the context of SOEs until the beginning of the century, when many contemporary SOEs have been deeply reformed in order to ensure greater transparency and accountability, and better compliance with ethical and deontological requirements (Picot et al. 2015, Bacchiocchi et al. 2019, Bernier et al. 2020b).

The theoretical framework is agency theory and the effectiveness of the board as an internal monitoring control to avoid technical and allocative inefficiencies and ultimately ensure wealth maximization to the shareholder (Jensen and Meckling, 1976). This framework is fully compatible with the one for private companies, with a similar emphasis on the role of the board and issues related to disclosure, transparency, and accountability. What is different is that SOEs may face two other distinct governance challenges: (1) they may suffer from undue hands-on and politically motivated ownership interference, which may prevent the governance of the SOE to autonomously define the goals and the strategy of the institutions without being influenced by the private agenda of politicians that may use SOEs to extract rents (Putniņš 2020, Parker 2021); (2) they may suffer from a lack of any oversight due to totally passive or distant ownership by the state, which may weaken the incentives of SOEs and their staff to perform in the best interest of

Table 2 Selected papers from the empirical literature on the corporate governance of SOEs (considering only SOEs)

Article	Dependent variable (Performance measure: productivity / profitability / innovation / environment / other)	Sample period	Geographical area	Industry	Corporate governance measures	Institutional quality, regulation, political factors (Control/moderator/no)	Estimation method	Corporate governance effect
Bozec & Dia (2007)	Productivity: technical efficiency	1976–2001	Canada	Cross-industry	Board size and independence	No	DEA model, OLS	Board size and board independence are positively related to firm technical efficiency
Menozzi et al. (2012)	Profitability: ROA; ROI; ROE	1994–2004	Italy	Local public utilities	Board composition	Control: political connections of board members	Dynamic panel data models	Negative effect of political connectedness of board
Grosman et al. (2019)	Other: level of investment (natural logarithms of capital expenditures on long-term fixed assets from cash-flow statements)	2000–2010	Russia	Cross-sector	Role of independent boards	No	OLS; GMM	Positive effect of independent boards
Sidki et al. (2024)	Performance: ROE, ROA, profit per employee	2011–2016	Germany	Utilities	Board composition – educational, management, and industry experience)	No	OLS	No significant results

the enterprise and the general public, and raise the likelihood of self-serving behaviour by corporate insiders (Grossi et al. 2015).

As outlined in Table 2, our selection of empirical papers identified four analyses on the corporate governance of SOEs.

Bozec and Dia (2007) investigate the board–performance relationship for a sample of cross-industry Canadian SOEs. The authors scrutinize the impact of independence on the firms' technical efficiency measured using non-parametric data envelopment analysis and find a positive relation, meaning that SOEs with a larger proportion of outsiders on their board and fewer public servants are more likely to be associated with a higher performance. Similarly, Menozzi et al. (2012) focus on board composition, defined in terms of outsiders as opposed to insiders and, among the outsiders, distinguishing between politically connected directors versus independent directors. They find that politically connected directors (i.e., those who are currently holding a seat in the parliament or in the municipal, provincial, or regional government or have held one in the past) exert a significant inflationary effect on employment while the opposite holds for the independent directors, who exercise a disciplinary role on labour demand and prevent SOEs to be over-employed. The composition of the board is also analyzed in Grosman et al. (2019), who investigate the role of independent directors in mitigating blockholders' mismanagement of funds and appropriation of firm wealth at the expenses of minority shareholders and creditors (so-called 'blockholder appropriation'). The authors focus on Russia, which only recently adopted corporate governance practice such as the presence of independent directors, and find that the presence of independent directors is associated with a reduction of blockholder appropriation, and that this is more accentuated in SOEs than in private firms. The authors attribute the difference in the influence of independent directors across ownership types to SOEs going through a much more thorough selection process in the nomination of their independent directors, and to the declared effort to curtail corruption.

Sidki et al. (2024) move away from the internal versus outsider/independent trade-off and focus on skills and competences of politically connected board directors. The authors analyze the biographical information (i.e., education, management experience, industry experience) of board members of a sample of state-owned utility German companies and find statistically significant differences between politically connected and non-political members, especially with regards to management and industry expertise. However, despite the lower level of business competence among politically connected board members, the estimation results indicate no relevant influence of these factors on the financial performance of the analyzed utility companies. According to the authors, it may be the case that the influence of supervisory boards among SOEs is relatively weak in the German framework, where decision-making power lies in bodies outside the typical construct of corporate governance such as municipal councils.

By highlighting that board composition is positively related to firm efficiency, results from this recent body of literature are quite consistent with regulatory reforms adopted by several countries in line with the Principles of Corporate Governance for State-Owned Enterprises set by the OECD in 2015 (OECD 2015a,b)[9], whose main message is that the board is chiefly responsible for setting the corporate strategy and major plans of action, monitoring the implementation of the strategy and the achievement of the goals, ensuring the integrity of the corporation's accounting and financial reporting system, safeguarding independent audit, control, and compliance (Iwu-Egwuonwu 2010, Pargendler et al. 2013, Tremml 2019, Vining and Laurin 2020).

This issue is strictly related to the problem of *time consistency*, which arises whenever the effectiveness of a policy today depends on the credibility of the commitment to implement that policy in the future, and which requires a credible obligation of the state to guarantee the autonomy of SOEs, that in turn can be improved by taking all the precautions and providing all the incentives that are needed to ensure that the SOEs' mission is sufficiently internalized by the managers (OECD 2020). In turn, a strong and well-defined public mission can attract staff with a specific intrinsic public service motivation and altruism. As highlighted in Section 2.8, this stream of literature is mainly theoretical (Francois and Vlassopoulos 2008, Polidori and Teobaldelli 2013, Willner and Grönblom 2020), while empirical research is still scant and not specifically related to SOEs, and offers few and sometimes contradictory evidence regarding these effects (Papenfuß and Keppeler 2020, Jacobsen 2021).

Alternatively, empirical analyses may also treat corporate governance as the dependent variable and assess how it is influenced by state ownership. This is the focus of analysis in Borisova et al. (2012), which concludes that government ownership is generally detrimental to the corporate governance of European firms, particularly in the context of civil law systems. However, more empirical research is needed to test to what extent the guidelines on corporate governance are actually followed and their effects. It would be crucial to assess whether SOEs are progressively aligning with international best standards and to investigate whether these developments, if any, have the intended effects on the effectiveness of SOEs in achieving their objectives. Conducting such empirical

---

[9] In 2023 the OECD began a review of the Guidelines to reflect evolving best practices and to ensure that SOEs contribute to sustainability, and economic security and resilience, by maintaining a global level playing field and high standards of integrity and business conduct. The OECD conducted a public consultation on revisions to the Guidelines in July–September 2023; the new Guidelines are expected to be published by end 2024.

studies will not only contribute to a deeper understanding of the evolving landscape of SOEs but also provide insights into the impact of their adherence to international standards, their public involvement, and the awareness about its mission and management from citizens, who ultimately 'own' SOEs.

3.6 The Aggregate Effect of State Ownership

As documented above, SOEs are still active players in the economy, producing goods and services, going abroad, and performing deals in the M&A market. They also play a role in innovation and some societal goals. Ownership matters for performance and productivity, although the actual net effect is different across sectors, countries, and institutional settings, and highly dependent upon empirical methods. Against this backdrop, what is the overall effect of public ownership at the aggregate level?

Table 3 presents a selection of empirical papers on the impact of SOEs on the aggregate economy.

Earlier literature focused on employment effects, highlighting the role of SOEs as employers, especially in declining industries or in times of crises (see e.g., Svejnar (1996) for Eastern Europe and Bognetti (2020) for a historical perspective). However, Feldmann (2006), in an analysis of the relation between government size and unemployment, finds that the larger the share of public investment in SOEs, the greater the level of unemployment, especially for some categories of workers, casting doubts on this channel of aggregate impact of SOEs. Szarzec et al. (2021) analyze the link between the economic weight of SOEs, measured by the share of state-owned total assets, operating revenues, and employment of large non-financial enterprises in each country, and growth in Europe between 2007 and 2016. Their main result is that the presence of SOEs is not positive or negative per se on economic growth, but is mediated by institutional quality, with a high percentage of SOEs having beneficial effects on growth only when the institutional setting is good. A possible mechanism through which SOEs may positively impact aggregate economic performance and growth is related to their role in knowledge creation and as vehicles of social objectives. Evidence on the former mechanism is provided, for example, by Antonelli et al. (2014) who consider the case of economic growth in Italy between 1950 and 1994 and show that R&D that was conducted in SOEs had a greater impact on country level TFP growth than private R&D. With respect to the latter, instead, Avsar et al. (2013) document the existence of a U-shaped relationship between the size of the SOE sector, measured by the share of the SOE sector production in GDP, and national inequality (Gini coefficient) in the 1970–2004 period worldwide. For low levels of inequality, the correlation between inequality and the size of SOEs is positive, while for high levels of

Table 3 Review of the empirical literature on the SOEs' impact to the aggregate economy

Article	Dependent variable	Sample period	Geographical area	Industry	Institutional quality, regulation, political factors (Control/ moderator/ no)	SOE measure (Dichotomous / discrete / continuous)	Estimation method	State ownership effect (Positive / negative / not significant / mixed)
Feldmann (2006)	Aggregate unemployment data	1985–2002	19 industrialized countries		Control: labour market institutions	Continuous: size of public sector	GLS	negative
Avsar et al. (2013)	Relative size of the SOEs in overall economic activity (GDP)	1970–2004	World		Control & moderator: political ideology	Continuous	2SLS	Mixed (inverted U-shape relationship between inequality and size of SOE sector)
Antonelli et al. (2014)	TFP growth (country level)	1950–1994	Italy		No	Dichotomous (IRI)	OLS/dynamic panel data models	Positive
Adua & Clark (2021)	Environment / innovation (energy efficiency)	2016	U.S.A.	Largest electric utilities	Actually, the main variables: political factors	Continuous (not properly SOE, but political factors; two measures: (1) % Republicans in state Congressional Delegation to 113th U.S. Congress; (2) No. of years Republican held governor's office, 2009–2014)	Structural equation modelling, cluster-robust standard errors	Negative (but depending on the dominating party: Republican vs. Democratic)
Szarzec et al. (2021)	GDP growth	2007–2016	Europe		Moderator	Discrete: majority SOE, minority SOE, private	GMM	Positive conditional on institutional quality

Bridgman and Greenaway-McGrevy (2022)	Log difference of labour share (LS); log difference of wage inequality	1960–2010	OECD countries	Cross-industry (aggregate at the country level)	No	Continuous: log difference of public employment share	Long run (5-year, 10-year, 15-year, 20-year horizon intervals) OLS; TWFE	Mixed (overstaffing, in terms of higher LS, but redistribution to the working class, in terms of lower wage inequality)

inequality the reverse is true. The authors also analyze the role of political ideology in shaping this relationship, providing additional evidence of the importance of context conditions when considering the impact of ownership on economic activities in general.

4 Concluding Remarks

This Element contributes to the economic literature on contemporary SOEs, with a focus on developed market economies, from two perspectives: normative and positive. There are important differences between these perspectives, and misunderstanding can arise from the lack of convergence in modelling and interpretation of data when empirics is not guided by theory.

In this final section we summarize our findings and directly compare the research questions arising from economic theory with the answers given by empirical literature in the last twenty years.

First of all, there is an issue in defining what an SOE is. We suggest that the most appropriate concept, an ideal-type, is an organization with managerial autonomy, own budget, a public mission ultimately, controlled by one or jointly more than one government, which could, in principle, be privatized. In empirical analyses a formalistic definition is often adopted, and the public mission ingredient is largely overlooked. The practical consequence is, for example, that an oil & gas corporation with no other objective than rent maximization for the investors, either public or private, is considered in the same category as an SOE tasked by the government to manage the energy transition away from fossil fuels. We argue that performance cannot be compared if objectives are not assessed in the first place.

Clearly, in the abstract framework of the first theorem of welfare economics it is immaterial who owns a firm – whether an individual or jointly by all the citizens represented by a government agency: profit maximization would be Pareto efficient in a Walras equilibrium. Hence, there is no proper role for SOEs. In fact, from an empirical perspective, many contemporary SOEs without a public mission, competing with similar POEs, achieve – *ceteris paribus* – the same profitability performance, as one might expect.

The previous theory of SOEs in public economics, about fifty years ago, was concerned with pricing rules under monopoly. However, monopolistic SOEs (or state-invested companies) are now rather an exception. In some cases, they are the incumbents in regulated industries, and much of the previous literature on Ramsey pricing or other rules no longer applies in this context. Unfortunately, most of the empirical literature on SOE profitability not only adopts a formalistic definition but also fails to systematically control for market dominance to explain the outcomes.

Moreover, from a normative perspective, observed prices – whether regulated or arising from imperfect competition – cannot be taken at face value as the marginal social value of outputs and inputs. Unfortunately, the use of shadow prices for evaluating public investment through SOEs in sectors such as in energy, water, transport, health, research infrastructures is unsystematic. While ex-ante CBA is used when governments make investment decisions, comparable ex-post data are lacking. Thus, we know something about the financial profitability of SOEs and something about CBA of investment, but not about their actual performance in terms of economic profitability (shadow profits) just because the data are not available.

The same issue is relevant for the extensive literature on productivity. In most cases, output is not measured against production factors, but rather through proxies based on revenue and cost values, which are in turn defined through possibly distorted prices, with the same problems of empirical profitability analysis.

With all the limitations arising from the mismatch of normative and positive analysis, a clear message from the empirical literature in the last twenty years is that the quality of government matters for SOE productivity. This finding conveys a more constructive message than the one arising from the earlier theoretical literature on bureaucracy and government capture in the public choice tradition. SOEs are in fact efficient, even in the standard way to measure efficiency, when they operate in a healthy institutional environment. Any empirical cross-country model omitting a quality of government variable would lead to biased estimated coefficients, as it would attribute to SOEs an underperformance that is not directly caused by government ownership but by some form of corruption of the decision process. This would apply to politically connected POEs as well. In our theoretical discussion, based on the Drèze-Stern CBA framework, we have argued that policy distortions destroy the validity of shadow prices as marginal social values for evaluation (while this is not the case for inefficient production plans). This is also evident in the theoretical discussion by Laffont (2005) and in similar models when politicians and managers are self- interested. In such circumstances, the issue is how to improve government (which includes law-making and the judiciary) and not just SOEs.

A concern of earlier theoretical literature is the concept of soft-budget constraint for SOEs, that would harm taxpayers and competitors. While this was relevant for Soviet-type economies, there is limited evidence that it is also relevant for SOEs in developed market economies (China is a different story), even if occasionally it is likely that soft loans from public financial institutions bailed out SOEs. However, this happened for POEs as well (General Motors and Chrysler, two US-based car makers are notable examples), thus it is not clear that the case against SOEs can be argued because they attract subsides, soft loans, or other incentives more than any other large-scale company (including public procurement for construction, oil & gas, pharma, defence, etc.). Moreover, there are theoretical models that suggest that in some case restrictions on discontinuation of bad projects may be an incentive to better project screening in the first place if information is asymmetric, because of the ex-post cost of 'white elephants'. Clearly, more empirical research is needed on this issue.

Another under-researched topic is the outcome of mixed oligopoly. While the theoretical literature is now taking advantage from more than thirty years of work (reviewed in another Element in this series, *Mixed Oligopoly and Public Enterprises* by Joanna Poyago-Theotoky), the empirics is less developed. It would however be important to see if it is true, as predicted by the mixed oligopoly literature, that SOE have different objectives than POE in such markets, and to what extent this leads to lower prices, higher quality, more innovativeness, more environmental sustainability than in purely POE oligopolies.

In a behavioural economics perspective, the notion of 'homo economicus' is dismissed and a stream of literature points to theoretical models where organizations with public missions or not-for-profit tend to attract people with intrinsic motivation and altruism. In our normative definition of SOEs, if these theories have merit, we would expect to see that the stronger the public mission, the greater the attraction of motivated staff. This question would require appropriate empirical methods (such as quasi-experiments) to be applied for example to public vs private hospitals, schools, research organizations, but also to utilities and other services of general interest where POEs and SOEs (in a variety of legal forms) co-exist.

Finally, the empirical literature on SOEs often overlooks the implications of endogenous growth theory, particularly regarding the suboptimal R&D expenditures by POEs. This issue, confirmed by abundant evidence, has led governments to invest in creating entirely new types of public enterprises focused on knowledge creation. While CBA of research infrastructures is in its infancy, there is some evidence that a large share of the approximately 8.8 million R&D personnel in the world (UNESCO 2021) are directly or indirectly involved in producing or using knowledge, especially as open science provided by these organizations. This underscores their importance in offering a new perspective on SOEs, including their role in knowledge creation for energy transition and climate change, human and animal health, digital transition, space economy, and other frontier policy issues.

All of this would require a solid governance framework for a new generation of SOEs, and we have reviewed sensible recommendations suggested notably by the OECD. More empirical research is needed to test the extent to which these guidelines are actually followed and their effects. An issue less present in the current literature is public involvement and awareness about SOEs. This is only imperfectly addressed by the obligation for SOEs in some jurisdictions to publish special reports on sustainability and corporate social responsibility. At a more fundamental level, the concern is to what extent citizens perceive that they 'own' SOEs and what voice they have to check or influence their missions and management. This is another topic for future research on SOEs and potentially for policy implications regarding their accountability and governance.

References

* Full references appearing in Tables 1, 2 and 3.

Abadie, A., Drukker, D., Herr, J. L. & Imbens, G. (2004). Implementing matching estimators for average treatment effects in Stata. *Stata Journal*, 4, 290–311.

Abadie, A. & Imbens, G. (2011). Bias-corrected matching estimators for average treatment effects. *Journal of Business & Economic Statistics*, 29, 1–11.

Abbot, M. & Cohen, B. (2009). Productivity and efficiency in the water industry. *Utilities Policy*, 17, 233–244.

Ackerberg, D. A., Caves, K. & Frazer, G. (2015). Identification properties of recent production function estimators. *Econometrica*, 83(6), 2411–2451.

* Adua, L. & Clark, B. (2021). Politics and corporate-sector environmentally significant actions: the effects of political partisanship on US utilities energy efficiency policies. *Review of Policy Research*, 38(1), 31–48.

* Aguilera, R., Duran, P., Heugens, P. P. M. A. R., Sauerwald, S., Turturea, R. & VanEssen, M. (2021). State ownership, political ideology, and firm performance around the world. *Journal of World Business*, 56(1), 101113.

Alesina, A. & Tabellini, G. (2004). *Bureaucrats or Politicians?* CEPR Discussion Paper no. 4252.

Andreoni, J. (1990). Impure altruism and donations to public goods: a theory of warm-glow giving. *The Economic Journal*, 100(401), 464–477.

* Antonelli, C., Amidei, F. B. & Fassio, C. (2014). The mechanisms of knowledge governance: state owned enterprises and Italian economic growth, 1950–1994. *Structural Change and Economic Dynamics*, 31, 43–63.

Arora, A., Belenzon, S. & Patacconi, A. (2017). The decline of science in corporate R&D. *Strategic Management Journal*, 39(1), 3–32.

* Asaftei, G., Kumbhakar, S. C. & Mantescu, D. (2008). Ownership, business environment and productivity change. *Journal of Comparative Economics*, 36(3), 498–509.

Atkinson, A. B. & Stiglitz, J. E. (1980). *Lectures on Public Economics*. New York: McGraw Hill. Updated edition: 2015, Princeton, NJ: Princeton University Press.

* Avsar, V., Karayalcin, C. & Ulubasoglu, M. A. (2013). State-owned enterprises, inequality, and political ideology. *Economics and Politics*, 25(3), 387–410.

Bacchiocchi, E., Ferraris, M., Florio, M. & Vandone, D. (2019). State-owned banks in the market for corporate control. *Journal of Economic Policy Reform*, 22(2), 120–147.

* Bacchiocchi, E., Florio, M. & Gambaro, M. (2011). Telecom reforms in the EU: prices and consumers' satisfaction. *Telecommunications Policy*, 35(4), 382–396.

* Backx, M., Carney, M. & Gedajlovic, E. (2002). Public, private and mixed ownership and the performance of international airlines. *Journal of Air Transport Management*, 8(4), 213–220.

Bai, C. E., Li, D. D., Tao, Z. & Wang, Y. (2000). A multitask theory of state enterprise reform. *Journal of Comparative Economics*, 28(4), 716–738.

Bai, W. & Wang, Y. (2022). Optimal mechanism in governmental project screening: a theory of Kornai's soft budget constraint. *Journal of Government and Economics*, 7, 1–8.

Bayliss, K. & Fine, B. (1998). Beyond bureaucrats in business: a critical review of the World Bank approach to privatization and public sector reform. *Journal of International Development*, 10(7), 841–855.

Bel, G. & Calzada, J. (2009). Privatization and universal service obligations. *Journal of Institutional and Theoretical Economics (JITE) / Zeitschrift Für Die Gesamte Staatswissenschaft*, 165(4), 650–669.

Belloc, F. (2014). Innovation in state-owned enterprises: reconsidering the conventional wisdom. *Journal of Economic Issues*, 48(3), 821–848.

* Ben-Nasr, H. (2016). State and foreign ownership and the value of working capital management. *Journal of Corporate Finance*, 41, 217–240.

Bénabou, R. & Tirole, J. (2006). Incentives and prosocial behavior. *American Economic Review*, 96(5), 1652–1678.

Benassi, M. & Landoni, M. (2019). State-owned enterprises as knowledge-explorer agents. *Industry & Innovation*, 26(2), 218–241.

* Benito, G. R., Rygh, A. & Lunnan, R. (2016). The benefits of internationalization for state-owned enterprises. *Global Strategy Journal*, 6(4), 269–288.

Berndt, E. R. & Christensen, L. R. (1973). The translog function and the substitution of equipment, structures and labor in U.S. manufacturing, 1929–1968. *Journal of Econometrics*, 1, 81–114.

Bernier, L., Florio, M. & Bance, P. (2020a). Introduction. In L. Bernier, M. Florio & P. Bance, eds., *The Routledge Handbook of State-Owned Enterprises*. London: Routledge, pp. 1–22.

Bernier, L., Florio, M. & Bance, P. (2020b). *The Routledge Handbook of State-Owned Enterprises*. London: Routledge.

Bertero, E. & Rondi, L. (2002). Does a switch of budget regimes affect investment and managerial discretion of state-owned enterprises? Evidence from Italian firms. *Journal of Comparative Economics*, 30(4), 836–863.

Besley, T. (2006). *Principled Agents? The Political Economy of Good Government*, New York: Oxford University Press.

Besley, T. & Gathak, M. (2005). Competition and incentives with motivated agents. *American Economic Review*, 95(3), 616–636.

* Beuselinck, C., Cao L., Deloof, M. & Xia, X. (2017). The value of government ownership during the global financial crisis. *Journal of Corporate Finance*, 42, 481–493.

Bianchi, P. (2012). *Dizionario di Economia e Finanza*. Rome: Treccani.

* Biggar, D. & Söderberg, M. (2020). Empirical analysis of how political ideology and ownership influence price stability in the Swedish district heating market. *Energy Policy*, 145, 111759.

* Boardman, A. E., Vining, A. R. & Weimer, D. L. (2016). The long-run effects of privatization on productivity: evidence from Canada. *Journal of Policy Modelling*, 38(6), 1001–1017.

Bognetti, G. (2020). History of western state-owned enterprises: from the Industrial Revolution to the age of globalization. In L. Bernier, M. Florio & P. Bance, eds., *The Routledge Handbook of State-Owned Enterprises*. London: Routledge, pp. 25–44.

* Boitani, A., Nicolini, M. & Scarpa, C. (2013). Do competition and ownership matter? Evidence from local public transport in Europe. *Applied Economics*, 45(11), 1419–1434.

Boiteux, M. (1956). Sur la gestion des monopoles publics astreints à l'équilibre budgétaire. *Econometrica*, 24(1), 22–40.

* Borghi, E., Del Bo, C. & Florio, M. (2016). Institutions and firms' productivity: evidence from electricity distribution in the EU. *Oxford Bulletin of Economics and Statistics*, 78(2), 170–196.

Borisova, G., Brockman, P., Salas, J. & Zagorchev, A. (2012). Government ownership and corporate governance: evidence from the EU. *Journal of Banking and Finance*, 36, 2917–2934.

* Borisova, G., Fotak, V., Holland, K. & Megginson, W. (2015). Government ownership and the cost of debt: evidence from government investments in publicly traded firms. *Journal of Financial Economics*, 118, 168–191.

* Bortolotti, B., Fotak, V. & Wolfe, B. (2019). Innovation at State-Owned Enterprise, Working Paper, University of Turin and University at Buffalo.

* Bozec, R. & Dia, M. (2007). Board structure and firm technical efficiency: evidence from Canadian state-owned enterprises. *European Journal of Operational Research*, 177(3), 1734–1750.

* Bozec, R., Dia, M. & Breton, G. (2006). Ownership-efficiency relationship and the measurement selection bias. *Accounting and Finance*, 46(5), 733–754.
* Brau R., Doronzo R., Fiorio C. & Florio M. (2010). EU gas industry reforms and consumers' prices. *The Energy Journal*, 31(4), 167–182.
* Bridgman, B. & Greenaway-McGrevy, R. (2022). Public enterprise and the rise and fall of labor share. *Economic Inquiry*, 60(1), 320–350.

Bruton, G. D., Peng, M. W., Ahlstrom, D., Stan, D. & Xu, K. (2015). State-owned enterprises around the world as hybrid organizations. *The Academy of Management Perspectives*, 29(1), 92–114.

* Calza, F., Profumo, G. & Tutore, I. (2016). Corporate ownership and environmental proactivity. *Business Strategy and the Environment*, 25(6), 369–389.
* Calzada, J. & Diaz-Serrano, L. (2023). Conflicting national policies: the creation of the euro and the rebalancing of telecommunications prices. *Telecommunications Policy*, 47(1), 102458.
* Castelnovo, P. (2022). Innovation in private and state-owned enterprises: a cross-industry analysis of patenting activity. *Structural Changes and Economic Dynamics*, 62, 98–113.
* Castelnovo, P., Del Bo, C. F. & Florio, M. (2019). Quality of institutions and productivity of state-invested enterprises: international evidence from major telecom companies. *European Journal of Political Economy*, 58, 102–117.

CEEP (2010). *Public Services in the European Union and in the 27 Member States: Statistics, Organization and Regulations*. Study commissioned in the framework of the "Mapping of the Public Services" project managed by CEEP.

Ceriani, L. & Florio, M. (2011). Consumer's surplus and the reform of network industries: a primer. *Journal of Economics*, 102(2), 111–122.

Chambers, R. G. (1988). *Applied Production Analysis*. Cambridge: Cambridge University Press.

Chan, K. K. Y., Chen, L. & Wong, N. (2018). New Zealand state-owned enterprises: is state-ownership detrimental to firm performance? *New Zealand Economic Papers*, 52(2), 170–184.

* Chen, V. Z., Musacchio, A. & Li, S. (2018). A principals-principals perspective of hybrid leviathans: cross-border acquisitions by state-owned MNEs. *Journal of Management*, 45(7), 2751–2778

Christiansen, H. (2013). *Balancing Commercial and Non-Commercial Priorities of State-Owned Enterprises*. OECD Corporate Governance Working Papers, No. 6. Paris: OECD Publishing.

Christensen, T. & Lægreid, P. (2011). Complexity and hybrid public administration: theoretical and empirical challenges. *Public Organization Review*, 11(4), 407–423.

Christiansen, H. & Kim, Y. (2014). *State-Invested Enterprises in the Global Marketplace: Implications for a Level Playing Field*. OECD Corporate Governance Working Papers, No. 14. Paris: OECD Publishing.

Clifton, J., Comín, F. & Fuentes, D. D. (2003). *Privatisation in the European Union: Public Enterprises and Integration*. London: Springer Science & Business Media.

Clifton, J., Comín, F. & Fuentes, D. D. (2006). Privatizing public enterprises in the European Union 1960–2002: ideological, pragmatic, inevitable? *Journal of European Public Policy*, 13(5), 736–756.

Clifton, J., Fuentes, D. D. & Warner, M. (2016). The loss of public values when public shareholders go abroad. *Utilities Policy*, 40, 134–143.

Clò, S., Del Bo, C. F., Ferraris, M., Florio, M., Vandone, D. & Fiorio, C. (2015). Public enterprises in the market for corporate control: recent worldwide evidence. *Annals of Public and Cooperative Economics*, 86(4), 559–583.

* Clò, S., Ferraris, M. & Florio, M. (2017a). Ownership and environmental regulation: evidence from the European electricity industry. *Energy Economics*, 61, 298–312.

* Clò S., Fiorio C. V. & Florio M. (2017b). The targets of state capitalism: evidence from M&A deals. *European Journal of Political Economy*, 47, 61–74.

* Clò, S., Florio, M. & Rentocchini, F. (2020). Firm ownership, quality of government and innovation: evidence from patenting in the telecommunication industry. *Research Policy*, 49(5), 103960.

Clò, S., Frigerio, M. & Vandone, D. (2022). Financial support to innovation: the role of European development financial institutions. *Research Policy*, 51(10), 104566.

Comin, D. (2010). Total factor productivity. In S. N. Durlauf & L. E. Blume., eds., *Economic Growth*. London: Palgrave Macmillan, pp. 260–263.

Cornett, M. M., Lin Guo, S. K. & Hassan, T. (2010). The impact of state ownership on performances differences in privately-owned versus state-owned banks: an international comparison. *Journal of Financial Intermediation*, 19, 74–94.

* Coulomb, R. & Sangnier, M. (2014). The impact of political majorities on firm value: do electoral promises or friendship connections matter? *Journal of Public Economics*, 115, 158–170.

* Dal Bo, E. & Rossi, M. A. (2007). Corruption and inefficiency: theory and evidence from electric utilities. *Journal of Public Economics*, 91, 939–962.

* Dalen, D. M. & Gómez-Lobo, A. (2003). Yardsticks on the road: regulatory contracts and cost efficiency in the Norwegian bus industry. *Transportation*, 30, 371–386.

de Chaisemartin, C. & D'Haultfoeuille, X. (2020). Two-way fixed effects estimators with heterogeneous treatment effects. *American Economic Review*, 110(9), 2964–2996.

de Chaisemartin, C. & D'Haultfoeuille, X. (2023). Two-way fixed effects and differences-in-differences with heterogeneous treatment effects: a survey. *The Econometrics Journal*, 26(3), C1–C30.

De Fraja, G. & Delbono, F. (1990). Game theoretic models of mixed oligopoly. *Journal of Economic Surveys*, 4(1), 1–17.

* De Lange, B. & Merlevede, B. (2020). State-Owned Enterprises Across Europe: Stylized Facts From a Large Firm-level Dataset. Ghent University, Faculty of Economics and Business Administration.

De Loecker, J., Goldberg, P. K., Khandelwal, A. K. & Pavcnik, N. (2016). Prices, markups, and trade reform. *Econometrica*, 84(2), 445–510.

* Del Bo, C., Ferraris, M. & Florio, M. (2017). Governments in the market for corporate control: evidence from M&A deals involving state-owned enterprises. *Journal of Comparative Economics*, 45(1), 89–109.

Del Bo, C. & Florio, M. (2012). Public enterprises, planning and policy adoption: three welfare propositions. *Journal of Economic Policy Reform*, 15(4), 263–279.

* del-Río, B., Fernández-Sainz, A. & de Alegria, I. M. (2019). Industrial electricity prices in the European Union following restructuring: a comparative panel-data analysis. *Utilities Policy*, 60, 100956.

Dewatripont M. & Maskin, E. (1995). Credit and efficiency in centralized and decentralized economies. *Review of Economic Studies*, 62(4), 541–556.

* Dewenter, K. L. & Malatesta, P. H. (2001). State-owned and privately owned firms: an empirical analysis of profitability, leverage, and labor intensity. *American Economic Review*, 91(1), 320–334.

Diamond, P. A. & Mirrlees, J. A. (1971a). Optimal taxation and public production I: production efficiency. *American Economic Review*, 61(1), 8–27.

Diamond, P. A. & Mirrlees, J. A. (1971b). Optimal taxation and public production II: tax rules. *American Economic Review*, 61(3), 261–278.

* Díaz, G. & Charles, V. (2016). Regulatory design and technical efficiency: public transport in France. *Journal of Regulatory Economics*, 50(3), 328–350.

Doherty, B., Haugh, H. & Lyon, F. (2014). Social enterprises as hybrid organizations: a review and research agenda. *International Journal of Management Reviews*, 16(4), 417–436.

Drèze J. & Stern N. (1990). Policy reform, shadow prices, and market prices. *Journal of Public Economics*, 42(1), 1–45.

* Driffield, N. L., Mickiewicz, T. & Temouri, Y. (2013). Institutional reforms, productivity and profitability: from rents to competition? *Journal of Comparative Economics*, 41(2), 583–600.

D'Souza, J. & Nash, R. (2017). Private benefits of public control: evidence of political and economic benefits of state ownership. *Journal of Corporate Finance*, 46, 232–247.

* Earnhart, D. & Lizal, L. (2006). Effects of ownership and financial performance on corporate environmental performance. *Journal of Comparative Economics*, 34(1), 111–129.

* Eller, S. L., Hartley, P. R. & Medlock, K. B. (2011). Empirical evidence on the operational efficiency of national oil companies. *Empirical Economics*, 40, 623–643.

Eslava, M. & Freixas, X. (2021). Public development banks and credit market imperfections. *Journal of Money Credit and Banking*, 53(5), 1121–1149.

Estrin S., Hanousek J., Kočenda E. & Svejnar J. (2009). The effects of privatization and ownership in transition economies. *Journal of Economic Literature*, 47(3), 699–728.

* Estrin, S., Meyer, K. E., Nielsen, B. B. & Nielsen, S. (2016). Home country institutions and the internationalization of state-owned enterprises: a cross-country analysis. *Journal of World Business*, 51(2), 294–307.

Estrin, S. & Pelletier, A. (2018). Privatization in developing countries: what are the lessons of recent experience? *The World Bank Research Observer*, 33(1), 65–102.

EU (2021). *EU consultation on 'Sustainable Corporate Governance'* 26/10/2020–8/2/2021.

European Commission (2018). *Action Plan: Financing Sustainable Growth* COM(2018) 97 final. Brussels, 8/3/2018.

European Commission (2020). *Study on directors' duties and sustainable corporate governance*.

* Feldmann, H. (2006). Government size and unemployment: evidence from industrial countries. *Public Choice*, 127(3–4), 443–459.

Florio, M. (2004). *The great divestiture. Evaluating the welfare impact of the British privatisations 1979–1997*. Cambridge, MA: The MIT Press.

Florio, M. (2006). Una teoria positiva delle privatizzazioni per i paesi in via di sviluppo: note a margine delle ultime lezioni di Jean Jacques Laffont. *Politica Economica*, 23, 131–156.

Florio, M. (2013). *Network industries and social welfare: the experiment that reshuffled European utilities*. Oxford: Oxford University Press.

Florio, M. (2019). *Investing in science: social cost–benefit analysis of research infrastructures*. Cambridge: MA, MIT Press.

* Fiorio, C. V. & Florio, M. (2011). Would you say that the price you pay for electricity is fair? Consumers' satisfaction and utility reforms in the EU15. *Energy Economics*, 33(2), 178–187.

* Fiorio, C. V. & Florio, M. (2013). Electricity prices and public ownership: evidence from the EU15 over thirty years. *Energy Economics*, 39(C), 222–232.

Florio, M., Gamba, S. & Pancotti, C. (2023). *Mapping of long-term public and private investments in the development of Covid-19 vaccines*. European Commission, Directorate-General for Internal Policies, IPOL_STU(2023) 740072.

Florio, M. & Pancotti, C. (2023). *Applied welfare economics: cost–benefit analysis of projects and policies*. 2nd edn. London: Routledge.

Francois, P. (2000). 'Public service motivation' as an argument for government provision. *Journal of Public Economics*, 78(3), 275–299.

Francois P. & Vlassopoulos M. (2008). Pro-social motivation and the delivery of social services. *CESifo Economic Studies*, 54(1), 22–54.

Frigerio, M. & Vandone, D. (2020). European development banks and the political cycle. *European Journal of Political Economy*, 62, 101852.

Gil-Moltó, M. J., Poyago-Theotoky, J., Rodrigues-Neto, J. A., & Zikos, V. (2020). Mixed oligopoly, cost-reducing research and development, and privatisation. *European Journal of Operational Research*, 283(3), 1094–1106.

Gil-Moltó, M. J., Poyago-Theotoky, J., & Zikos, V. (2011). R&D subsidies, spillovers, and privatization in mixed markets. *Southern Economic Journal*, 78(1), 233–255.

* Goldeng, E., Grünfeld, L. A. & Benito, G. R. G. (2008). The performance differential between private and state-owned enterprises: the roles of ownership, management and market structure. *Journal of Management Studies*, 45(7), 1244–1273.

Goldstein, A. (2013a). Big Business in the BRICs. *The Handbook of Global Companies*, pp. 53–74.

Goldstein, A. (2013b). The political economy of global business: the case of the BRICs. *Global Policy*, 4(2), 162–172.

* Grøgaard, B., Rygh A. & Benito, G. R. (2019). Bringing corporate governance into internalization theory: state ownership and foreign entry strategies. *Journal of International Business Studies*, 50, 1310–1337.

Grönblom, S. & Willner, J. (2014). Organisational form and individual motivation: public ownership, privatisation and fat cats. *Journal of Economic Policy Reform*, 17(3), 267–284.

* Grosman, A., Aguilera, R. V. & Wright, M. (2019). Lost in translation? Corporate governance, independent boards and blockholder appropriation. *Journal of World Business*, 54(4), 258–272.
Grossi, G., Papenfuß, U. & Tremblay, M.-S. (2015). Corporate governance and accountability of state-owned enterprises: relevance for science and society and interdisciplinary research perspectives. *International Journal of Public Sector Management*, 28(4–5), 274–285.
* Growitsch, C. & Stronzik, M. (2014). Ownership unbundling of natural gas transmission networks: empirical evidence. *Journal of Regulatory Economics*, 46, 207–225.
* Growitsch, C. & Wetzel, H. (2009). Testing for economies of scope in European railways: an efficiency analysis. *Journal of Transport Economics and Policy*, 43(1), 1–24.
Guiso, L., Sapienza, P. & Zingales, L. (2004). The role of social capital in financial development. *American Economic Review*, 94(3), 526–556.
Gupta, N. (2005). Partial privatization and firm performance. *Journal of Finance*, 60, 987–1015.
Hansmann, H. (2000). *The ownership of enterprise*. Cambridge, MA: Harvard University Press.
Hefetz, A. & Warner, M. (2004). Privatization and its reverse: explaining the dynamics of the government contracting process. *Journal of Public Administration Research and Theory*, 14(2), 171–190.
Hefetz, A. & Warner, M. (2011). Contracting or public delivery? The importance of service, market and management characteristics. *Journal of Public Administration Research and Theory*, 22(2), 289–317.
Hellman, J. S., Jones, G. & Kaufmann, D. (2003). Seize the state, seize the day: state capture and influence in transition economies. *Journal of Comparative Economics*, 31(4), 751–773.
Henisz, W. J. (2000). The institutional environment for economic growth. *Economics and Politics*, 12, 1–31.
Henisz, W. J. (2002). The institutional environment for infrastructure investment. *Industrial and Corporate Change*, 11, 355–389.
Hindriks, J., & Claude, D. (2006). Strategic privatization and regulation policy in mixed markets. *The IUP Journal of Managerial Economics*, 4(1), 7–26.
Hindriks, J. & Myles, G. D. (2013). *Intermediate Public Economics*. Cambridge, MA: MIT press.
Holland, K. (2019). Are all government owners viewed the same? Evidence from government acquisitions of publicly traded firms. *Journal of Corporate Finance*, 56, 319–352.

Hood, C. (1995). The 'new public management' in the 1980s: variations on a theme. *Accounting, Organisations and Society*, 20(2–3), 93–109.

IMF (2020) Fiscal Monitor, https://www.imf.org/en/Publications/FM/Issues/2020/04/06/fiscal-monitor-april-2020, accessed July 8, 2022.

* Inoue, C. (2020). Election cycles and organizations: how politics shapes the performance of state-owned enterprises over time. *Administrative Science Quarterly*, 65(3), 677–709.

* Inoue, C. F., Lazzarini, S. G. & Musacchio, A. (2013). Leviathan as a minority shareholder: firm-level implications of state equity purchases. *Academy of Management Journal*, 56(6), 1775–1801.

Iwu-Egwuonwu, R. C. (2010). Some empirical literature evidence on the effects of independent directors on firm performance. *Journal of Economics and International Finance*, 2(9), 190–198.

Jacobsen D. (2021). Motivational differences? Comparing private, public and hybrid organizations. *Public Organization Review*, 21, 561–575

Jamasb, T. & Pollitt, M. (2011). Electricity sector liberalisation and innovation: an analysis of the UK's patenting activities. *Research Policy*, 40(2), 309–324.

Jamasb, T. & Pollitt, M. (2015). Why and how to subsidise energy R&D: lessons from the collapse and recovery of electricity innovation in the UK. *Energy Policy*, 83, 197–205.

James, H. S. (2005). Why did you do that? An economic examination of the effects of extrinsic compensation on intrinsic motivation and performance. *Journal of Economic Psychology*, 26, 549–566.

* Jaslowitzer, P., Megginson W. & Rapp, M. (2018). Disentangling the Effects of State Ownership on Investment – Evidence from Europe. Working Paper, University of Oklahoma.

Jensen, M. & Meckling, W. H. (1976). Theory of the firm: managerial behavior, agency costs and ownership structure. *Journal of Financial Economics*, 3(4), 305–360.

Johansson, P. O. & Kriström, B. (2018). *Cost–benefit analysis*. Elements in Public Economics. Cambridge: Cambridge University Press.

* Jory, S. R. & Ngo, T. N. (2014). Cross-border acquisitions of state-owned enterprises. *Journal of International Business Studies*, 45, 1096–1114.

* Kabaciński, B., Kubiak, J. & Szarzec, K. (2020). Do state-owned enterprises underperform compared to privately owned companies? An examination of the largest polish enterprises. *Emerging Markets Finance and Trade*, 56(13), 3174–3192.

* Kalasin, K., Cuervo-Cazurra, A. & Ramamurti, R. (2020). State ownership and international expansion: the S-curve relationship. *Global Strategy Journal*, 10(2), 386–418.

* Karolyi, G. A. & Liao, R. C. (2017). State capitalism's global reach: evidence from foreign acquisitions by state-owned companies. *Journal of Corporate Finance*, 42, 367–391.

Kaufmann, D., Kraay, A. & Mastruzzi, M. (2010). *The worldwide governance indicators: methodology and analytical issues*. World Bank Policy Research Working Paper, No. 5430.

Koppell, J. G. S. (2003). *The Politics of Quasi-Government: Hybrid Organizations and the Dynamics of Bureaucratic Control*. Cambridge: Cambridge University Press.

Kornai J. (1980). *Economics of Shortage*. Amsterdam: North-Holland.

Kornai, J. (1992). *The Socialist System. The Political Economy of Communism*. Oxford: Oxford University Press.

Kornai, J. (2001). Hardening the budget constraint: the experience of the post-socialist countries. *European Economic Review*, 45(9), 1573–1599.

Koske, I., Wanner, I., Bitetti, R. & Barbiero, O. (2015). *The 2013 Update of the OECD's Database on Product Market Regulation: Policy Insights for OECD and Non-OECD Countries*. OECD Economics Department Working Papers, No. 1200. Paris: OECD Publishing.

Kowalski P., Büge, M., Sztajerowska M. & Egeland, M. (2013). *State-Owned Enterprises, Trade Effects and Policy Implications*. OECD Trade Policy Papers, No. 147. Paris: OECD Publishing.

Kwiatkowski, G., Mroczek, J. & Golebiowska, M. (2023). How much of the world economy is state-owned? Analysis based on the 2005–20 Fortune Global 500 lists. *Annals of Public and Cooperative Economics*, 94(2), 659–677.

* Kwoka Jr., J. E. (2005). The comparative advantage of public ownership: evidence from U.S. electric utilities. *Canadian Journal of Economics*, 38(2), 622–640.

Laffont, J. J. (2005). *Regulation and Development*. Cambridge: Cambridge University Press.

Laffont J. J. & Tirole J. (1993). *A Theory of Incentives in Procurement and Regulation*. Cambridge, MA: The MIT Press.

* Lazzarini, S. G., Mesquita, L. F., Monteiro, F. & Musacchio, A. (2021). Leviathan as an inventor: an extended agency model of state-owned versus private firm invention in emerging and developed economies. *Journal of International Business Studies*, 52, 560–594.

* Lazzarini, S. G. & Musacchio A. (2018). State ownership reinvented? Explaining performance differences between state-owned and private firms. *Corporate Governance: An International Review*, 26(4), 255–272.

Lazzarini, S. G., Musacchio, A., Bandeire-De-Mello, R. & Marcon, R. (2015). What do state- owned development banks do? Evidence from BNDES, 2002–2009. *World Development*, 66, 237–253.

Lee, S. H., & Hwang, H. S. (2003). Partial ownership for the public firm and competition. *The Japanese Economic Review*, 54(3), 324–335.

* Le Lannier, A. & Porcher, S. (2014). Efficiency in the public and private French water utilities: prospects for benchmarking. *Applied Economics*, 46(5), 556–572.

Levinsohn, J. & Petrin, A. (2003). Estimating production functions using inputs to control for unobservables. *The Review of Economic Studies*, 70(2), 317–341.

Lin, J. Y. (2021). State-owned enterprise reform in China: the new structural economics perspective. *Structural Change and Economic Dynamics*, 58, 106–111.

Lin, K. J., Lu, X., Zhang, J. & Zheng, Y. (2020). State-owned enterprises in China: a review of 40 years of research and practice. *China Journal of Accounting Research*, 13(1), 31–55.

Lipsey, R. (2007). Reflections on the general theory of second best at its golden jubilee. *International Tax and Public Finance*, 14(4), 349–364.

Marois T. (2022). A dynamic theory of public banks (and why it matters). *Review of Political Economy*, 34(2), 356–371.

Maskin, E. S. (1996). Theories of the soft-budget constraint. *Japan and the World Economy*, 8(2), 125–133.

Matsumura, T. (1998). Partial privatization in mixed duopoly. *Journal of Public Economics*, 70(3), 473–483.

Megginson, W. L. (2005). *The Financial Economics of Privatization*. New York: Oxford University Press.

Megginson, W. L. (2016). Privatization, state capitalism, and state ownership of business in the 21st century. *Foundations and Trends in Finance*, 11(1–2), 1–153.

Megginson, W. L. & Liu, X. (2022). State ownership and corporate governance. In M. Wright, G. T. Wood, A. Cuervo-Cazurra, P. Sun, I. Okhmatovsky & A. Grosman, eds., *The Oxford Handbook of State Capitalism and the Firm*. Oxford: Oxford University Press, pp. 131–165.

Megginson, W. L. & Netter, J. (2001). From state to market: a survey of empirical studies on privatization. *Journal of Economic Literature*, 39(2), 321–389.

Meissner, D., Sarpong, D. & Vonortas, N. (2019). Introduction to the special issue on innovation in state owned enterprises: implications for technology

management and industrial development. *Industry and Innovation*, 26(2), 121–126.
* Menozzi, A., Gutiérrez Urtiaga, M. & Vannoni, D. (2012). Board composition, political connections, and performance in state-owned enterprises. *Industrial and Corporate Change*, 21(3), 671–698.
* Meyer, A. & Pac, G. (2013). Environmental performance of state-owned and privatized eastern European energy utilities. *Energy Economics*, 36, 205–214.

Milhaupt, C. J. (2020). The state as owner – China's experience. *Oxford Review of Economic Policy*, 36(2), 362–379.

Millward, R. (2007). *Private and public enterprise in Europe: energy, telecommunications and transport, 1830–1990* (Cambridge Studies in Economic History – Second Series). Cambridge: Cambridge University Press.

Millward, R. (2013). *The State and Business in the Major Powers. An Economic History 1815–1939*. London: Routledge.

Miroudot, S. & Ragoussis, A. (2011). Actors in the international investment scenario: objectives, performance and advantages of affiliates of state-owned enterprises and sovereign wealth funds. In R. Echandi & P. Sauvé, eds., *Prospects in International Investment Law and Policy*. World Trade Forum, pp. 51–72.

Mühlenkamp, H. (2015). From state to market revisited: a reassessment of the empirical evidence on the efficiency of public (and privately-owned) enterprises. *Annals of Public and Cooperative Economics*, 86(4), 535–557.

Musacchio, A., Lazzarini, S. G. & Aguilera, R. V. (2015). New varieties of state capitalism: strategic and governance implications. *Academy of Management Perspectives*, 29(1), 115–131.

Newbery, D. M. (2000). *Privatization, Restructuring and Regulation of Network Utilities, (The Walras-Pareto Lectures, 1995)*. Cambridge, MA: The MIT Press.

Niskanen, W. (1971). *Bureaucracy & Representative Government*. Chicago: Aldine-Atherton.

Nölke, A. (Ed.) (2014). *Multinational Corporations From Emerging Markets: State Capitalism 3.0*. Basingstoke: Palgrave Macmillan.

North, D. C. (1991). Institutions. *Journal of Economic Perspectives*, 5(1), 97–112.

OECD (2006). OECD Guidelines on Corporate Governance of State-owned Enterprises, in *Corporate Governance of State-Owned Enterprises: A Survey of OECD Countries*. Paris: OECD Publishing.

OECD (2014). *The Size and Sectoral Distribution of SOEs in OECD and Partner Countries*. Paris: OECD Publishing.

OECD (2015a). *Guidelines on Corporate Governance of State-Owned Enterprises*. Paris: OECD Publishing.

OECD (2015b). *Principles of Corporate Governance*. Paris: OECD Publishing.

OECD (2017). *The Size and Sectoral Distribution of State-Owned Enterprises*. Paris: OECD Publishing.

OECD (2020). *Implementing Guidelines on Corporate Governance of State-Owned Enterprises: Review of Recent Developments*. Paris: OECD Publishing.

OECD (2021). *Ownership and Governance of State-Owned Enterprises: A Compendium of National Practices 2021*. Paris: OECD Publishing.

OECD (2024). *Recommendation of the Council on Guidelines on Corporate Governance of State-Owned Enterprises*, OECD/LEGAL/0414. Paris: OECD Publishing.

Olley, G. & Pakes, A. (1996). The dynamics of productivity in the telecommunications equipment industry. *Econometrica*, 64(6), 1263–1297.

Oum, T., Adler N. & Yu C. (2006). Privatization, corporatization, ownership forms and their effects on the performance of the world's major airports. *Journal of Air Transport Management*, 12(3), 109–121.

Papenfuß, U. & Keppeler, F. (2020). Does performance-related pay and public service motivation research treat state-owned enterprises loke a neglected Cinderella? A systematic literature review and agenda for future research on performance effects. *Public Management Review*, 22(7), 1119–1145.

Pargendler, M., Musacchio, A. & Lazzarini, S. (2013). In strange company: the puzzle of private investment in state-controlled firms. *Cornell International Law Journal*, 46, 569.

Parker, D. (2021). Privatization of State-Owned Enterprises. *Oxford Research Encyclopedia of Business and Management*. Oxford: Oxford University Press.

Picot, A., Florio, M., Grove, N. & Kranz, J. (2015). *The Economics of Infrastructure Provisioning. The Changing Role of the State*. Cambridge, MA: The MIT Press.

Polidori, P. & Teobaldelli, D. (2013). Prosocial behavior in the production of publicly provided goods and services: an overview. *International Review of Applied Economics*, 27(2), 285–296.

Poyago-Theotoky, J. (2024). *Mixed Oligopoly and Public Firms*. Cambridge Elements in Public Economics. Cambridge: Cambridge University Press.

Putniņš, T. J. (2020). Economics of state-owned enterprises. In L. Bernier, M. Florio & P. Bance, eds., *The Routledge Handbook of State-Owned Enterprises*. London: Routledge, pp. 215–238.

* Qingyuan L., Lin C. & Xu L. (2020). Political investment cycles of state-owned enterprises. *Review of Financial Studies*, 33, 3088–3129.

Robinson, W. I. (2015). The transnational state and the BRICS: a global capitalism perspective. *Third World Quarterly*, 36(1), 1–21.

Rodrik, D. & Stantcheva, S. (2021). *Oxford Review of Economic Policy*, 37(4), 824–837.

Roland, G. (2008). *Privatization: Successes and Failures*. New York: Columbia University Press.

Romer, P. M. (1990). Endogenous technological change. *Journal of Political Economy*, 98(5, pt.2), S71–S102.

Roodman, D. (2009). How to do xtabond2: an introduction to difference and system GMM in Stata. *Stata Journal*, 9(1), 86–136.

* Roy, W. & Yvrande-Billon, A. (2007). Ownership, contractual practices and technical efficiency: the case of urban public transport in France. *Journal of Transport Economics and Policy*, 41(2), 257–282.

Sappington, D. E. & Sidak, J. G. (2003). Incentives for anticompetitive behavior by public enterprises. *Review of Industrial Organization*, 22(3), 183–206.

* Scheffler, R., Hartwig, K. H. & Malina, R. (2013). The effects of ownership structure, competition, and cross-subsidisation on the efficiency of public bus transport: empirical evidence from Germany. *Journal of Transport Economics and Policy*, 47(3), 371–386.

* Sidki, M., Boerger, L. & Boll, D. (2024). The effect of board members' education and experience on the financial performance of German state-owned enterprises. *Journal of Management and Governance*, 28, 445–482.

Sjåfjell B. (2018). Redefining the corporation for a sustainable new economy. *Journal of Law and Society*, 45(1), 29–45.

Slawinski, N., Pinkse, J. Busch, T. & Banerjeed, S. B. (2017). The role of short-termism and uncertainty in organizational inaction on climate change: multilevel framework. *Business and Society*, 56(2), 253–282.

Sorrentino, M. (2020). State-owned enterprises and the public mission: A multidimensional lens. In L. Bernier, M. Florio & P. Bance, eds., *The Routledge Handbook of State-Owned Enterprises*. London: Routledge, pp. 73–90.

* Sterlacchini, A. (2012). Energy R&D in private and state-owned utilities: an analysis of the major world electric companies. *Energy Policy*, 41, 494–506.

* Stiel, C., Cullmann, A. & Nieswand, M. (2018). Do private utilities outperform local government-owned utilities? Evidence from German retail electricity. *German Economic Review*, 19(4), 401–425.

Stiglitz, J. (1994). *Whither Socialism?* Cambridge, MA: The MIT Press.

* Suárez-Varela, M., García-Valiñas, M. A., González-Gómez, F. & Picazo-Tadeo, A. J. (2017). Ownership and performance in water services revisited: does private management really outperform public? *Water Resources Management*, 31(8), 2355–2373.

Svejnar, J. (1996). Enterprises and workers in the transition: econometric evidence. *The American Economic Review*, 86(2), 123–127.

Sykes J. B. (1982). *The Concise Oxford Dictionary of Current English*, 7th edn. Oxford: Clarendon Press.

* Szarzec, K., Dombi, Á. & Matuszak, P. (2021). State-owned enterprises and economic growth: evidence from the post-Lehman period. *Economic Modelling*, 99, 105490.

* Szarzec, K. & Nowara, W. (2017). The economic performance of state-owned enterprises in Central and Eastern Europe. *Post-Communist Economies*, 29(3), 375–391.

Thynne, I. (2021). State-Owned Enterprises: Structures, Functions, and Legitimacy. *Oxford Research Encyclopedia of Politics*. Oxford: Oxford University Press.

Tihanyi, L., Aguilera, R. V., Heugens, P., van Essen, M., Sauerwald, S., Duran, P. & Turturea, R. (2019). State ownership and political connections. *Journal of Management*, 45(6), 2293–2321.

Tonin, M. & Vlassopoulos, M. (2010). Disentangling the sources of pro-socially motivated effort: a field experiment. *Journal of Public Economics*, 94(11–12), 1086–1092.

Toninelli, P. (2011). *The Rise and Fall of State-Owned Enterprise in the Western World*. Cambridge: Cambridge University Press.

Tõnurist, P. (2015). Framework for analyzing the role of state-owned enterprises in innovation policy management: the case of energy technologies and EestiEnergia. *Technovation*, 38, 1–14.

Tõnurist, P. & Karo, E. (2016). State-owned enterprises as instruments of innovation policy. *Annals of Public and Cooperative Economics*, 87(4), 623–648.

Tremml, T. (2019). Linking two worlds? Entrepreneurial orientation in public enterprises: a systematic review and research agenda. *Annals of Public & Cooperative Economics*, 90(1), 25–51.

UNESCO Science Report. (2021). The race against time for smarter development. S. Schneegans, T. Straza and J. Lewis (eds). UNESCO Publishing: Paris.

Van Beveren, I. (2012). Total factor productivity estimation: a practical review. *Journal of Economic Surveys*, 26, 98–128.

Van Biesebroek, J. (2008). The sensitivity of productivity estimates: revisiting three important debates. *Journal of Business and Economic Statistics*, 26, 311–328.

Vickers J. & Yarrow G. (1988). *Privatization: An Economic Analysis*, Cambridge, MA: The MIT Press.

Vining, A. R., Boardman, A. E. & Moore, M. A. (2014). The theory and evidence pertaining to local government mixed enterprises. *Annals of Public and Cooperative Economics*, 85(1), 53–86.

Vining, A. R. & Laurin, C. (2020). State-owned enterprise hybrids. In L. Bernier, M. Florio & P. Bance, eds., *The Routledge Handbook of State-Owned Enterprises*. London: Routledge, pp. 413–430.

Vining, A. R. & Weimer, D. L. (2016). The challenge of fractionalized property rights in public-private hybrid organizations: the good, the bad, and the ugly. *Regulation & Governance*, 10(2), 161–178.

Vining, A. R. & Weimer, D. L. (2017). Debate: Adam Smith was skeptical of hybrids—should we be less so? *Public Money & Management*, 37(6), 387–388.

Walter, M., Cullmann, A., von Hirshhausen, C., Wand, R. & Zschille, M. (2009). Quo vadis efficiency analysis of water distribution? A comparative literature review. *Utilities Policy*, 17, 225–232.

Willner, J. (2001). Ownership, efficiency, and political interference. *European Journal of Political Economy*, 17(4), 723–748.

Willner, J. (2010). *Public Options and Altruistic Firms-Antitrust Targets or Tools? The Welfare Impact of a Mixed Oligopoly with Managerial firms*. Discussion paper No. 59. Aboa Centre for Economics.

Willner, J. & Grönblom, S. (2020). Motivation and performance in state-owned enterprises. In L. Bernier, M. Florio & P. Bance, eds., *The Routledge Handbook of State-Owned Enterprises*. Routledge, pp. 282–300.

* Wolf, C. (2009). Does ownership matter? The performance and efficiency of State Oil vs. Private Oil (1987–2006). *Energy Policy*, 37(7), 2642–2652.

World Bank (1994). *Bureaucrats in Business: The Economics and Politics of Government Ownership Dataset*. World Bank Policy Research Report. Oxford: Oxford University Press for the World Bank.

Cambridge Elements

Public Economics

Robin Boadway
Queen's University

Robin Boadway is Emeritus Professor of Economics at Queen's University. His main research interests are in public economics, welfare economics and fiscal federalism.

Frank A. Cowell
The London School of Economics and Political Science

Frank A. Cowell is Professor of Economics at the London School of Economics. His main research interests are in inequality, mobility and the distribution of income and wealth.

Massimo Florio
University of Milan

Massimo Florio is Professor of Public Economics at the University of Milan. His main interests are in cost-benefit analysis, regional policy, privatization, public enterprise, network industries and the socio-economic impact of research infrastructures.

About the Series

The Cambridge Elements of Public Economics provides authoritative and up-to-date reviews of core topics and recent developments in the field. It includes state-of-the-art contributions on all areas in the field. The editors are particularly interested in the new frontiers of quantitative methods in public economics, experimental approaches, behavioral public finance, empirical and theoretical analysis of the quality of government and institutions.

Cambridge Elements

Public Economics

Elements in the Series

The Role of the Corporate Tax
Roger Gordon and Sarada

Behavioral Science and Public Policy
Cass R. Sunstein

Empirical Fiscal Federalism
Federico Revelli and Emanuele Bracco

Economic Principles of Commodity Taxation
Vidar Christiansen and Stephen Smith

The Economics and Regulation of Network Industries with Applications to Telecommunications
Ingo Vogelsang

The Public Economics of Changing Longevity
Pierre Pestieau

Tax Policy: Principles and Lessons
Robin Boadway and Katherine Cuff

Political Competition and the Study of Public Economics
Stanley L. Winer and J. Stephen Ferris

Benefit–Cost Analysis of Air Pollution, Energy, and Climate Regulations
Kerry Krutilla and John D. Graham

The Economics of Social Protection
Pierre Pestieau

Mixed Oligopoly and Public Enterprises
Joanna Poyago-Theotoky

State-Owned Enterprises in Developed Market Economies: Theory and Empirics
Chiara F. Del Bo, Massimo Florio, Marco Frigerio and Daniela Vandone

A full series listing is available at: www.cambridge.org/PEC

For EU product safety concerns, contact us at Calle de José Abascal, 56–1°,
28003 Madrid, Spain or eugpsr@cambridge.org.

www.ingramcontent.com/pod-product-compliance
Lightning Source LLC
LaVergne TN
LVHW020349260326
834688LV00045B/1626